D0536000

At My
Grandmother's Knee

Faye Porter

THOMAS NELSON
Since 1798

NASHVILLE   DALLAS   MEXICO CITY   RIO DE JANEIRO

*I dedicate this book to Grandma Ferkan and Grandma Porter;
my mum; my aunts: Lois, Wilma, Sara, Margaret, Emma,
Esther, Helen, Sue, Jane, Max, and Shirley; and all the women
in my life who have shared with me the joy of cooking, baking,
loving, making a home, and giving from their hands and hearts.
And to my priceless nieces: Lillian, Ava, Olivia, and Sophia—
may you always be surrounded by such love and joy.*

*Special thanks to Bryan, Joe, Chip, Violet, Kelly, Lauren,
Mandy, and Chloe—your help has been priceless.*

Published in Nashville, Tennessee, by Thomas Nelson. Thomas Nelson is a registered trademark of Thomas Nelson, Inc.

Edited by Heather Skelton

Photography by Ron Manville

Food styling by Teresa Blackburn

Page design by Walter Petrie

Image on page 32 by Alison Miksch, Brand X Pictures © Getty Images

Thomas Nelson, Inc., titles may be purchased in bulk for educational, business, fund-raising, or sales promotional use. For information, please e-mail SpecialMarkets@ThomasNelson.com.

Library of Congress Cataloging-in-Publication Data

Porter, Faye, 1966–
At my grandmother's knee / Faye Porter.
p. cm.
  ISBN 978-1-4016-0036-5
1. Cooking, American—Southern style. 2. Cookbooks. I. Title.
TX715.2.S68P67 2011
641.5975—dc22   2010042585

Printed in the United States of America

11 12 13 14 15 QGT 6 5 4 3

Contents

Introduction

You jump out of the car the second it's put into park. You think you closed the door behind you, but you're not really sure 'cause your heart is beating fast and you're beaming with excitement. You move up the stone walk as fast as your little legs and feet will take you and nearly collapse—into outstretched arms. Arms that pull you in and hold you with a closeness that surely feels like a little piece of heaven on earth. Arms and a heart overflowing with joy, pride, comfort, nurturing, and a love so sacred, pure, and unconditional that it could only be from your grandmother. And what does she need in return? The smile on your face as you enjoy a fresh-baked tea cake, as you lift your plate to ask for another helping of her chicken-fried steak, as you ask her to show you how to make her "famous" Southern sweet tea, or as you settle in to her big mushy chair for an afternoon nap with a peaceful look on your face. It's these simple, unspoken expressions of gratitude that make her life content.

Grandmothers continue to express their unique love for us with countless gestures throughout our lives. If we're lucky, we get to enjoy our grandmothers for a really long time. Some of us get to share our lives with them for only a short time—and we yearn for more details about them from older cousins, parents, or aunts and uncles who can help us fill in the missing pieces. Some of life's sweetest memories are centered around meals and rituals that over time become our family traditions. The moments that truly matter are the occasions when we are together and laughing, the times when our cheeks ache from smiling so much as we enjoy food prepared by the hands of those who love us the most. Even after a grandmother has passed on, we relive those memories anytime we smell a long-cooked roast or a particular brew of coffee, or see an almost velvet-like dark green pickle like she used to can, or taste a chocolate icing so dense and rich it could only be homemade. Especially in the South, so many memories are tied to food and its smell and taste. And, if we're open, we can learn so much about love and life from how it's prepared and served, and what it took for so many of those before us to do that day in and day out for their families because they didn't have convenient options. When times were lean, our Southern grandmothers gave what they had—fresh vegetables or fruit from their land, eggs and dairy from their chickens and cows, or meat from their husband's hunt. Or they prepared food and shared it by offering it to those in need or by hosting folks in their home. So much of what they knew and taught us about love and friendship started in their Southern kitchens.

And that brings us to this special book that I like to say is part cookbook and part history book, because it captures the love and guidance that so many of us soaked up from watching and listening to and asking questions of our Southern grandmothers as we helped them prepare a meal or bake for some special occasion. Recipes allow us to pass on the love and legacy of a grandma so she can be remembered, revered, and celebrated for generations to come. I hope you will enjoy the recipes and stories in the pages of this book. May they cause you to pause and fondly remember your grandmother or, if you're younger, think about the traditions you want to start that can be passed on to the next generation that can, when treasured, long outlive your lifetime.

FAYE PORTER

Breakfast

Granny's Sausage Gravy

Biscuits 'n' Chocolate Gravy

Sausage Biscuits

Nanny's Hash Brown Casserole

Brunch Casserole

Nanny's Morning Crepes

Grammy Gregg's Pan-Fried Mush

Southern Batter Pancakes

Blueberry Pancakes

Patsy's Chocolate-Chip Pancakes

Cowboy Coffee Cake

GRANNY'S SAUSAGE GRAVY

J. MARIE HEGLER (Mount Juliet, Tennessee) shares that you can't let her Granny's silver hair and diminutive stature fool you into thinking she is the typical "sweet little ol' grandma." Marie says, "While she is sweet, she is also the biggest jock in the family! She was very into competitive sports in high school and even played in leagues out of high school. Granny rules the TV remote. If there isn't a baseball game on to watch (particularly a Braves game), you will find her flipping the channels to see what other sports are on. There have even been desperate times when the main three sports were on hiatus and we've caught her watching soccer and golf." This Granny is **MARGARET POOLE EILAND** (Opp, Alabama).

I pound ground sausage

1/3 cup all-purpose flour

3 cups milk, divided

1/8 teaspoon Morton's Nature's Seasons

1 In a large skillet brown the sausage, but do not drain off the drippings.
2 In a large bowl whisk the flour with 1 cup of the milk until the lumps are gone.
3 Pour the milk and flour mixture into the skillet with the sausage and drippings. Stir well, add the remaining 2 cups milk, and sprinkle the seasoning on top. Stir and simmer until the texture is smooth. Serve over biscuits for breakfast.

MAKES 4 TO 6 SERVINGS.

BISCUITS 'N' CHOCOLATE GRAVY

SYLVIA DAVIS, known to her grandchildren as Ma, was born in Clay County, Tennessee, and later lived in Rutherford County. Granddaughter **SANDY JACKSON** (Hendersonville, Tennessee) shares that Ma sometimes made fried corn and fried chicken for breakfast! Sandy says, "Ma had particular bowls for mixing things such as bread and the best biscuits ever, and often did not use measuring cups or spoons. I've made Ma's chocolate gravy for my daughters since they were young—they love it so much, they still ask for it on special occasions, even as adults."

BISCUITS:
3 cups all-purpose flour

2 1/2 teaspoons baking powder

1/2 teaspoon baking soda

1/2 teaspoon salt

1/2 cup lard or shortening

I cup buttermilk

GRAVY:
1/2 stick butter

3/4 cup sugar

3 tablespoons all-purpose flour

1/3 cup cocoa

2 cups milk, divided

---

1 Preheat the oven to 450 degrees.

2 **TO MAKE THE BISCUITS**, combine the flour, baking powder, baking soda, and salt in a large bowl. Cut in the shortening using your hands and add the buttermilk.

3 Turn the dough out onto a floured work surface. Knead until smooth, adding additional flour if the dough is too sticky. Roll or pat the dough to 1/2-inch thick. Cut the dough into circles using a biscuit cutter. Place each biscuit on an ungreased cookie sheet.

4 Bake until golden brown, 10 to 12 minutes. Remove the biscuits from the oven and keep warm.

5 **TO MAKE THE GRAVY**, melt the butter in a cast-iron skillet over low heat. Mix in the sugar, flour, and cocoa. Add I cup of the milk and stir to keep lumps from forming. Slowly add the remaining I cup milk, stirring constantly so the mixture doesn't scorch. Serve warm on top of hot buttered biscuits or flapjacks.

MAKES 12 TO 15 BISCUITS.

❖❖❖ SAUSAGE BISCUITS

SHARONDA HAMPTON (Mount Juliet, Tennessee) shares that she and her sister called their dad's mother Maw-Maw or Little Maw-Maw. Maw-Maw was **MABLE MARY HILL WILLIAMS** and she was born and raised in Biloxi, Mississippi. Sharonda says, "When I was growing up, she lived next door to us and was really the only babysitter we ever knew. So many times we'd walk into her house to find her sitting at the counter with a big gray-speckled bowl, cutting up ingredients by hand with a silver paring knife for whatever she was planning to make."

I pound ground
sausage

2 cups all-purpose
flour

2 teaspoons baking
powder

I teaspoon salt

1/4 teaspoon baking
soda

1/2 cup shortening

3/4 cup buttermilk

1 Preheat the oven to 450 degrees.
2 In a skillet over medium heat, cook, drain, and crumble the sausage.
3 Sift together the flour, baking powder, salt, and baking soda in a medium bowl. Cut the shortening into the flour mixture. Stir in the sausage. Mix the buttermilk into the flour mixture.
4 Knead the dough by hand 10 times on a floured work surface. Roll the dough out to a 1/2-inch thickness. Cut out the biscuits with a biscuit cutter or the rim of a glass and place on an ungreased cookie sheet.
5 Bake for 10 minutes, or until golden brown. Serve warm.

MAKES 2 DOZEN BISCUITS.

NANNY'S HASH BROWN CASSEROLE

REBECCA BARBER (Smyrna, Tennessee) shares that her Nanny, **EVELYN DARBER** (Nashville, Tennessee), was a true Southern lady and very proper. She was a fanatic about her hair and got it done twice a week—people joked that she kept Aqua Net in business. Even though she appeared very proper to outsiders, her family never knew what to expect. Rebecca can't count the number of food fights that Nanny started. She was naturally funny and told the best stories—she kept her family in stitches.

2 pounds frozen hash brown potatoes

1 stick margarine, melted

1 can (10.75 ounces) cream of chicken soup

1 container (16 ounces) sour cream

1/2 cup chopped onion

2 cups shredded Cheddar cheese

1 teaspoon salt

1/4 teaspoon black pepper

cooking spray

1 Preheat the oven to 350 degrees.

2 In a large bowl combine the potatoes, margarine, soup, sour cream, onion, cheese, salt, and pepper and mix well.

3 Spray a 13 x 9-inch baking dish with cooking spray. Spoon the potato mixture into the baking pan.

4 Bake uncovered for 45 minutes, or until golden brown.

MAKES 6 TO 8 SERVINGS.

BRUNCH CASSEROLE

LINDSEY VASGAARD (Tallahassee, Florida) shares that her Nana, **BETTY VASGAARD** (Knoxville, Tennessee), got this recipe from her Nana Western. Nana Betty served this at her infamous "Betty's Bubbly Brunches" with sticky buns, cheese grits, and mimosas. Nana loved to have guests over—she was famous for her cooking and the huge meals she'd prepare when entertaining. Nana used to say, "Do you want some toast?"—no matter what your problem, sickness, or ailment was, Nana's solution was a toasted piece of her home-made sourdough bread.

4 cups cubed day-old bread (firm white or French)

2 cups shredded Cheddar cheese

10 large eggs

4 cups milk

I teaspoon dry mustard

1/4 teaspoon onion powder

1/8 teaspoon black pepper

9 slices bacon, cooked and crumbled

1/2 cup sliced fresh mushrooms

1/2 cup peeled and diced tomatoes

1 Preheat the oven to 325 degrees.

2 Arrange the bread in a greased 13 x 9-inch baking pan and sprinkle with the cheese.

3 Beat the eggs in a large bowl and mix in the milk, mustard, onion powder, and pepper.

4 Pour the egg mixture over the bread. Sprinkle with the bacon, mushrooms, and tomatoes.

5 Bake the casserole uncovered for 60 minutes, or until set. If the top starts to brown too early, tent the baking pan with foil and finish baking.

MAKES 8 TO 10 SERVINGS.

NOTE: *If you want to make this casserole the day before serving, you can cover it and refrigerate for up to 24 hours before baking.*

NANNY'S MORNING CREPES

LYNN WHITE (Tulsa, Oklahoma) shares that spending the night at the house of her Nanny, **DORIS MATTHEWS** (Birmingham, Alabama), meant she'd usually get homemade crepes for breakfast. "She used to tell me that many people eat them for dessert, but she liked to start her day with something sweet," Lynn recalls. "I never saw her in anything but a dress—usually with an apron over it—and she always wore little white socks rolled down around her ankles above her black tie shoes."

---

1 cup all-purpose flour

1 teaspoon sugar

1/2 teaspoon salt

2 large eggs

1 cup milk

1 tablespoon butter, melted

6 tablespoons apple butter or jelly (grape, strawberry, or other favorite)

powdered sugar for dusting

---

1 In a large bowl combine the flour, sugar, and salt. Add the eggs one at a time, beating well after each addition. Slowly add the milk to make a thin batter, beating until smooth. Stir in the melted butter. (Make sure the batter remains very thin—it should be thinner than pancake batter.)

2 Pour 1/2 cup of the batter onto a lightly greased skillet. Brown lightly on both sides. Repeat with the remaining batter. Spread the crepes with apple butter or your favorite jelly, roll up, and sprinkle with powdered sugar. Serve warm.

MAKES 6 SERVINGS.

GRAMMY GREGG'S PAN-FRIED MUSH

After traveling all over the country with a husband in the Coast Guard, Grammy ESTHER ELAINE FERKAN GREGG and her commander later settled in Lexington, Kentucky. She loved to cook and bake and you never left her house hungry, shares granddaughter LEIGH WILLHOIT DOUCET (Ruther Glen, Virginia). Leigh says, "She'd also make sunny-side-up eggs for our breakfast and call them 'dippy eggs.'"

---

2 3/4 cups water	I teaspoon salt	I tablespoon butter
I cup yellow cornmeal	I teaspoon sugar	

---

1 In a medium saucepan heat the water to boiling. Reduce the heat to medium and stir in the cornmeal, salt, and sugar. Cook, stirring frequently, until the mixture is thick.

2 Spoon the cornmeal mixture into a lightly greased 9 x 5-inch loaf pan. Cover and refrigerate overnight.

3 When ready to cook, melt the butter in a skillet over medium-high heat. Slice the mush into I-inch-thick slices. Cook the slices in the melted butter until golden brown on both sides. Serve with hot maple syrup.

MAKES 4 SERVINGS.

SOUTHERN BATTER PANCAKES

KATIE BRAMAN (Nashville, Tennessee) shares that her Mimi, **RUDELL BLALOCK** (Paducah, Kentucky), would always make these buttermilk pancakes for her and her sister and brother when they went to visit. And she would make them in the shape of bunny rabbits. Katie says, "As we all got older, she would let us make the bunny pancakes—it was the best part of our visit. To this day, even though all three of us are out of college, she still makes them for us!"

---

2 large eggs,
   separated

I cup buttermilk

2 tablespoons butter,
   melted

3/4 cups all-purpose
   flour

1/2 teaspoon baking
   soda

1/2 teaspoon double-
   acting baking
   powder

1/2 teaspoon salt

1/2 teaspoon sugar

---

1 Beat the egg whites until stiff. In a large bowl beat the egg yolks, add the buttermilk
   and melted butter, and mix well. In another large bowl, sift together the flour, baking
   soda, baking powder, salt, and sugar. Mix the flour mixture into the egg yolk and
   buttermilk mixture. Quickly fold in the stiffly beaten egg whites.

2 Drop the batter by heaping tablespoons onto a lightly greased hot griddle in a circle
   or your favorite shape. Turn when bubbly on one side. Cook on the other side to a
   golden brown and transfer to a hot platter. Serve with your favorite syrup or
   preserves, if desired.

MAKES ABOUT 18 PANCAKES.

BLUEBERRY PANCAKES

Mamaw **DEBORAH DOUTE** lives in Thompson's Station, Tennessee. Her young granddaughter, **LILI HARRIS** (Murfreesboro, Tennessee), shares that there's nothing better than spending the night at her Mamaw's house. Lili says, "In the mornings, she lets me help her cook breakfast. I get to crack the eggs and stir up the pancake batter. These are the best pancakes in the world!"

---

2 large eggs

1/2 cup sour cream

2 cups milk

2 2/3 cups all-purpose flour

2 tablespoons baking powder

2 tablespoons sugar

1/2 teaspoon salt

1/2 stick butter, melted

1 cup blueberries

vegetable oil for greasing the skillet or griddle

---

1 Beat the eggs in a large bowl and mix in the sour cream and milk. Add the flour, baking powder, sugar, and salt. Stir until the lumps disappear. Stir in the butter and fold in the blueberries.

2 Lightly grease a skillet or griddle with oil and place over medium heat. When hot, pour 1/4 cup of the batter onto the skillet. Flip the pancake when bubbles form on top, and cook until the second side is golden brown. Repeat with the remaining batter. Serve warm with your favorite syrup or preserves, if desired.

MAKES 20 TO 24 PANCAKES.

PATSY'S CHOCOLATE-CHIP PANCAKES

PAIGE SIMS (Franklin, Tennessee) calls her grandmother Patsy. Patsy is **PATSY CALDWELL** (Charlotte, Tennessee). Paige says, "Ever since I was a little girl and would spend the night, Patsy would always have chocolate-chip pancakes waiting for me in the kitchen when I woke up. She knew it was my favorite dish for breakfast. Chocolate chips and pancake ingredients became a staple in her pantry just in case I came to visit."

I ¼ cups self-rising flour

½ teaspoon baking soda

2 tablespoons sugar

I large egg

I cup buttermilk

3 tablespoons vegetable oil

½ cup miniature chocolate chips

vegetable oil for greasing the skillet or griddle

1 Sift together the flour, baking soda, and sugar in a large bowl. In a separate bowl, beat the egg and mix in the buttermilk and oil. Pour the egg mixture into the bowl with the flour mixture and stir just until blended. Add the chocolate chips and mix.

2 Lightly grease a skillet or griddle with oil and place over medium heat. When hot, pour ¼ cup of the batter onto the skillet. Flip the pancake when bubbles form on top, and cook until the second side is golden brown. Repeat with the remaining batter. Serve warm with your favorite syrup or preserves, if desired.

MAKES 8 TO 10 PANCAKES.

COWBOY COFFEE CAKE

Cowboy coffee cake says Sunday brunch to **AMY MAJORS** (Fort Worth, Texas). Her grandma, **EVELYN BROWN** (also of Fort Worth), would make the batter the night before. "On Sundays we'd all meet for church and then go back to Grandma's for family brunch," Amy says. "This coffee cake would smell so good baking while we set the table and helped Grandma get the rest of the meal together. Anytime I make it, the aroma takes me right back to Grandma's kitchen."

2 1/2 cups all-purpose flour

2 cups firmly packed brown sugar

1/2 teaspoon salt

2/3 cup shortening

1/2 teaspoon baking soda

2 teaspoons baking powder

1/2 teaspoon ground nutmeg

1/2 teaspoon ground cinnamon

1 cup buttermilk

2 large eggs

1 Preheat the oven to 375 degrees.

2 In a large bowl mix the flour, brown sugar, and salt. Cut in the shortening until the mixture is crumbly. Reserve 1/2 cup of the mixture for the topping. To the remaining mixture, add the baking soda, baking powder, nutmeg, and cinnamon and mix well. Add the buttermilk and eggs and mix well.

3 Pour the batter into 3 greased and floured 8-inch round cake pans. Top with the crumb mixture.

4 Bake for 25 to 30 minutes or until center tests done with a toothpick. Serve warm.

MAKES 6 TO 8 SERVINGS.

Bread-and-Butter Pickles (page 28) and *Mamaw's Pickles* (page 25)

Jams, Pickles, and Canning

Nanny's Peach Preserves
Spicy Peach Chutney
Blackberry Jam
Mamaw's Pickles
Red Cucumber Rings
Bread-and-Butter Pickles
Susie's Homemade Ketchup

NANNY'S PEACH PRESERVES

KATHERINE FINCH (Forrest City, Arkansas) shares that she and her three sisters fondly remember the bustle in their Nanny's basement at canning time. Nanny, **CLARA LILLIAN VERNON WADE** (Fort Smith, Arkansas), had a full-size kitchen in her basement—it was cool there (the house had no air-conditioning) and she could work long hours canning everything imaginable, getting things ready for the freezer or making jellies and jams. Katherine says, "Everything seemed so complicated to us as children, but we remember the love stirred into each bowl and placed into the canning jars. Everything was delicious that came from Nanny's basement!"

---

9 medium peaches (3 pounds)	3/4 cup water	4 pint jars, lids and rings
1 2/3 cups sugar	3 whole cloves	

---

1 Wash the peaches, peel them, and remove the pits. Cut the peaches into small slices.

2 In a large pot boil the sugar and water for 10 minutes, stirring occasionally. Add the peaches and cook, stirring quickly and constantly, until the liquid is transparent. Add the whole cloves while cooking.

3 Pour the preserves into hot, sterilized jars and seal them with the lids and rings.

4 Place the jars in a canner and keep them covered with at least 1 inch of water above the top of the jars. Keep the water boiling. Process the pint jars in the boiling-water bath for 35 minutes. Lift the jars out of the water and let them cool in a draft-free place—being careful not to touch or bump the jars while they sit. Allow to sit at least 12 hours. Once the jars are cool, you can check that they are sealed by verifying that the lid has been sucked down. Press gently in the center of the lid with your finger. If it pops up and down (often making a popping sound), it is not sealed. If you put the jar in the refrigerator right away, you can still use the contents. Only those jars that are properly sealed can be stored unrefrigerated.

MAKES 3 TO 4 PINTS.

SPICY PEACH CHUTNEY

JULIE EATON HELTSLEY (Tullahoma, Tennessee) is known by her only granddaughter, KATHERINE PAIGE HELTSLEY (Hendersonville, Tennessee), as Jules. Jules is known far and wide for her cooking and baking. She always makes huge meals and loves to entertain. Kate, her brother, and cousins love to spend the night with Jules and enjoy pancakes made the next morning with berries they picked the day before. The kids also enjoy helping Jules bring in veggies from the garden and seeing what she will make with them. She also bakes a mean peach and blackberry cobbler.

I tablespoon butter

I tablespoon minced garlic

2 shallots, minced

I medium jalapeño pepper, minced

3 cups peeled, chopped fresh peaches

1/2 cup golden raisins

1/4 cup sugar

I tablespoon cider vinegar

I tablespoon lemon juice

I teaspoon salt

1/2 teaspoon black pepper

I teaspoon hot sauce

1 In a small saucepan over medium heat, melt the butter. Add the garlic, shallots, and jalapeño and sauté until the garlic and onions are tender. Add the peaches and raisins and sauté for 2 to 3 minutes. Add the sugar, vinegar, lemon juice, salt, black pepper, and hot sauce.

2 Simmer for 10 to 15 minutes over low heat until the peaches are soft. Stir frequently, being careful not to let the mixture stick or burn. Serve at room temperature. You can store in the refrigerator for several days or use the hot-canning / water-bath method to extend the shelf life.

3 **TO CAN**, pour the mixture into sterilized pint jars, leaving $^1/4$ inch of space at the top. Add lids and tighten rings. Place jars in a canner and keep them covered with at least 1 inch of water above the top of the jars. Keep the water boiling. Process pint jars in the boiling-water bath for 35 minutes. Lift the jars out of the water and let them cool in a draft-free place—being careful not to touch or bump the jars while they sit. Allow to sit at least 12 hours. Once the jars are cool, you can check that they are sealed by verifying that the lid has been sucked down. Press gently in the center of the lid with your finger. If it pops up and down (often making a popping sound), it is not sealed. If you put the jar in the refrigerator right away, you can still use the contents. Only those jars that are properly sealed can be stored unrefrigerated.

MAKES 2 TO 3 CUPS.

BLACKBERRY JAM

"Putting up jam" with Granny, **ALMA MAE HUGHES DAVIS** (Clintwood, Virginia), was a summer tradition as far back as **MICHELLE FLEMING** (Nashville, Tennessee) can remember. Heading together to the berry patch behind her house, Granny would carry a stick to scare off snakes. Michelle recalls stuffing her mouth with berries when Granny wasn't looking—but somehow she always knew what her granddaughter was up to. Once back at home, Granny would cover Michelle's briar scratches and bug bites with pink calamine lotion. Michelle says that Granny included her in everything she did—planting and picking vegetables, berries, and flowers; rolling dough and cutting biscuits with a juice glass; sewing and quilting; art and music; and summer camping trips to Myrtle Beach, Tweetsie Railroad, and Gatlinburg. Granny broadened her world and shared her love of Appalachian culture.

---

6 cups crushed vine-ripened blackberries

I package (1.75 ounces) powdered pectin

8 cups sugar

12 pint jars, lids, and rings

---

1 Put the blackberries and pectin in a large pot. Cook over high heat, stirring constantly. Bring the mixture to a full boil. Stir in the sugar and bring to a hard boil for I minute.

2 Remove the pot from the stove and skim off the foam. Pour the jam into the pint canning jars, leaving 1/4 inch of space at the top. Place the lids on top of the jars and screw on the seals. Set the jars in boiling water for 10 minutes. Remove from the heat and let the jars cool in water for 5 minutes. Remove the jars and place them on a towel or cloth on the counter so they can continue to cool. Store in a cool, dry place. Refrigerate the jam after it's opened.

MAKES 12 PINTS.

ALISON HARRIS (Murfreesboro, Tennessee) shares that at age seventy-two, her Mamaw, **NAOMA MAINES** (Morehead, Kentucky), has more energy than she has at thirty-two! Mamaw works in her flower and vegetable gardens for hours every day. She lives by herself and keeps up everything in her own house, including her computer. She learned how to operate the computer on her own and can also troubleshoot when something goes wrong.

---

48 medium
cucumbers

1 gallon water

1/2 cup pickling salt

4 cups cider vinegar

4 half-gallon jars,
lids, and rings

2 large white onions,
thickly sliced

---

1 Wash the cucumbers, cut the ends off, and slice vertically.

2 Add the water, salt, and vinegar to a 2-gallon stainless steel pot. Cook over medium heat until the mixture boils and continue boiling for 10 minutes.

3 Stuff the jars with the cucumbers (about 12 vertical slices per jar). Carefully fill each jar to the top with the boiled solution and let it sit for 20 minutes. After 20 minutes dump the water back into the pot, leaving the pickles in the jar. Repeat this step a second and third time. After adding the solution for the third time, add a slice of onion to the top of each jar, making sure the onion slices are wide enough to cover the mouth of the jar. Seal each jar with a hot lid that has been boiled in water. After cooling the jars overnight, store them in a pantry, cellar, or other cool, dry place.

MAKES 4 HALF GALLONS.

RED CUCUMBER RINGS

MANDY HELTSLEY BUTTERS (Brentwood, Tennessee) remembers that MaMaw, **HELEN SPARKS NICHOLS** (Greenville, Kentucky), would sing songs to her and her siblings—the song that comes to mind is "Jolly Little Cookie Man." Mandy says, "She also had a huge screened-in porch—we'd play out there and pretend the porch was a cruise ship. My grandfather was a postman and he'd stop home for lunch. MaMaw would get in cahoots with us and hide, and we'd all try to 'scare' him when he walked in the door."

CUCUMBER RINGS:

16 pounds large
  cucumbers

8 ½ cups water

2 cups pickling lime

1 cup cider vinegar

1 ounce red food
  coloring

1 tablespoon alum

SYRUP:

3 ½ cups water

3 ½ cups cider
  vinegar

10 cups sugar, divided

8 cinnamon sticks

1 package (6 ounces)
  Red Hots candy

10 pint jars, lids, and
  rings

1 **TO MAKE THE CUCUMBER RINGS**, peel and slice the cucumbers 1-inch thick. Remove the seeds, making a ring from the cucumbers. Combine the water and pickling lime in a large bowl. Add the cucumbers, making sure there is enough water to cover them. Add more water if needed and let the cucumbers soak for 24 hours. Drain and wash the cucumbers thoroughly and soak them in a large bowl of ice water for 3 hours. Drain the cucumbers and put them in a large pot. Add the vinegar, red food coloring, and alum. Add enough water to cover the cucumbers and bring to a boil. Simmer for 2 hours, drain, and place in a large bowl.

2 **TO MAKE THE SYRUP**, in a large saucepan boil the water, vinegar, 7 cups of the sugar, cinnamon sticks, and Red Hots until the Red Hots dissolve.

3 Pour the syrup over the cucumbers, leaving in the cinnamon sticks. Let the mixture sit for 24 hours. Pour off the syrup and reboil the syrup in a saucepan, adding 1 cup of the sugar. Repour the syrup over the cucumbers and let the mixture sit covered for another 24 hours. Repeat this process for a total of 3 days, adding 1 cup of the syrup each day. On the third day, after boiling the syrup, skim off any foam and remove any remains of the cinnamon sticks (do not pour the syrup back into the bowl).

4 Place the cucumbers into the canning jars. Pour the syrup over the cucumbers. Place 1 new cinnamon stick into each jar and seal with the lids and rings while hot. Chill in the refrigerator before serving.

MAKES 10 PINTS.

BREAD-AND-BUTTER PICKLES

MARTHA BROWN LARKIN (Nashville, Tennessee) says that her Gran, **MARY ALMA ODOM SMARTT** (Cookeville, Tennessee), lived in her home while Martha was growing up and they used to cook together in the afternoons after school. Martha recalls, "As a child, I already had a type A personality and Gran always had to remind me not to 'work' the dough for the fried pies too much or not to mix the ingredients for the cake too long. She had such a gentle cooking hand—her pastries were so light and flaky and her cakes were a mile high!" Martha also remembers having these bread-and-butter pickles in quart jars in their kitchen cabinet for all the years that Gran was canning and living in their home. She has fond memories of being Gran's 'sous chef' with the assignment of cutting the cucumbers into little squares, the way Gran preferred to do it.

3 pounds cucumbers

1/3 cup kosher salt

5 cups cold water

1 2/3 cups sugar

2 cups cider vinegar

2 teaspoons prepared mustard

1 teaspoon celery seed

1/4 teaspoon turmeric

1/8 teaspoon mace

1 teaspoon ground ginger

3 medium onions, sliced thin

1/8 teaspoon crushed red pepper flakes

6 pint jars, lids, and rings

1 Wash the cucumbers, cut the ends off, and cut into small cubes.

2 In a large pot dissolve the salt in the water to make the brine. Add the cucumber cubes to the brine. Cover the pot and leave it in a cool place or in the refrigerator for 12 hours.

3 Combine the sugar and vinegar in another large pot and cook over medium heat until the sugar dissolves. Add the mustard and celery seed to the pot and stir. Add the turmeric, mace, ginger, and onions and stir again. Drain the cucumber pieces and add them to the pot. There should be enough liquid to cover the cucumbers. Cook over medium heat until the mixture comes to a boil. Turn down the heat and simmer for 5 minutes. Stir in the red pepper flakes and let the mixture cool in the pot for 3 hours.

4 Fill the pint canning jars with the pickles and seal with the canning lids and rings. Store in the refrigerator or can to store on the shelf.

5 TO CAN, place jars in a canner and keep them covered with at least 1 inch of water above the top of the jars. Keep the water boiling. Process pint jars in the boiling-water bath for 15 minutes. Lift the jars out of the water and let them cool in a draft-free place—being careful not to touch or bump the jars while they sit. Allow to sit at least 12 hours. Once the jars are cool, you can check that they are sealed by verifying that the lid has been sucked down. Press gently in the center of the lid with your finger. If it pops up and down (often making a popping sound), it is not sealed. If you put the jar in the refrigerator right away, you can still use the contents. Only those jars that are properly sealed can be stored unrefrigerated.

MAKES 6 PINTS.

SUSIE'S HOMEMADE KETCHUP

Author's note: This one is from my grandma, **SUSIE HENSEL FERKAN**. She was born in Pennsylvania to first-generation parents from what used to be known as Czechoslovakia. She was one of eight children. She had ten children of her own, so my three brothers and I were four of twenty-three grandchildren. Susie lived to be eighty years old. My memories of her are usually in her kitchen or on the back porch, with an apron over her dress and a really fine white hairnet.

---

1 peck tomatoes, very ripe (about 18 baseball-size tomatoes)*

6 medium green bell peppers, chopped

10 large onions, chopped

10 large apples, chopped

2 cups cider vinegar

3 teaspoons salt

2 ½ cups sugar

1 teaspoon ground cinnamon

1 teaspoon ground cloves

1 tablespoon paprika

4 pint jars with lids and seals

---

1 Core the tomatoes and slice into wedges. Put them in a large pot or Dutch oven. Add the peppers, onions, and apples. Cook over medium-low heat, stirring frequently, for 20 to 30 minutes—when the tomatoes cook down and the skins fall off, they are ready. (They need to be mushy enough to get good juice from a sieve or colander.)

2 Put a sieve or colander over a clean pot. Pour the cooked tomato, onion, and apple mixture over the sieve or colander. Continually press the contents into the colander to get all of the juice out. Discard the contents of the sieve or colander and keep all of the juice that has drained into the pot below.

3 To the pot add the vinegar, salt, sugar, cinnamon, cloves, and paprika. Cook the mixture over low to medium heat, stirring frequently until it thickens, for 1 to 2 hours, depending on how thick you like your ketchup.

---

* Roma tomatoes (also called paste tomatoes) work best because they have less surface area, thicker and meatier flesh, and less water. Beefsteak, Lemon Boy (yellow), or Better Boy varieties also work well. Make sure the tomatoes you choose are ripe but not mushy, bruised, or rotten.

4 When the ketchup is as thick as you like, pour the boiling hot mixture into sterilized jars, leaving $1/4$ inch of space at the top. When cool, store in the refrigerator. Alternatively, you can use the hot-canning / water-bath method to extend the shelf life.

5 **TO CAN**, place jars in a canner and keep them covered with at least 1 inch of water above the top of the jars. Keep the water boiling. Process pint jars in the boiling-water bath for 35 minutes. Lift the jars out of the water and let them cool in a draft-free place—being careful not to touch or bump the jars while they sit. Allow to sit at least 12 hours. Once the jars are cool, you can check that they are sealed by verifying that the lid has been sucked down. Press gently in the center of the lid with your finger. If it pops up and down (often making a popping sound), it is not sealed. If you put the jar in the refrigerator right away, you can still use the contents. Only those jars that are properly sealed can be stored unrefrigerated.

MAKES 3 TO 4 PINTS.

Beverages

Church–Day Punch
Southern Sweet Tea
Mema's Lemon Tea
Fruit Tea
Hot Spiced Tea

CHURCH-DAY PUNCH

Gran, **GRACE MAY CALHOUN** (Edmond, Oklahoma), was big on her faith, family, and friends. Every Sunday was church day, so if you were visiting Gran you'd be in church, remembers **ANNA TAYLOR** (Tulsa, Oklahoma). Anna says, "After church there were always cookies and homemade goodies and punch. I used to like to help Gran put the sherbet on top. And I remember her many times wiping the foamy mustache off my upper lip."

---

2 small envelopes (.23 ounces each) lemon or lime drink mix powder, unsweetened

2 cups sugar

4 cups cold water

1 can (46 ounces) pineapple juice, chilled

1 bottle (2 liters) lemon-lime soda, chilled

1 pint lime or rainbow sherbet

---

1 Put the drink mix and sugar in a large bowl or punch bowl. Add the water and pineapple juice and stir until the drink mix and sugar dissolve. Chill in the refrigerator until ready to serve.

2 Right before serving, add the soda and stir. Spoon in the sherbet so that it floats on top. You can also add a colored frozen ice mold to help keep the punch cold, if desired.

MAKES 8 TO 10 SERVINGS.

SOUTHERN SWEET TEA

COURTNEY HINTON (Hermitage, Tennessee) loves Southern sweet tea! And both of her grandmas did too. Her maternal grandma, Nanny, is **MARTHA WRIGHT** (Nashville, Tennessee) and her paternal grandma was **EVELYN HINTON** (also of Hermitage). Mimi was the name that Courtney used for Evelyn. When Courtney's mom makes this sweet tea, for a different twist she sometimes uses a spearmint-flavored tea bag when steeping the tea.

2 quarts water

2 family-size tea bags
(or 4 regular-size bags)

3/4 cup sugar

1/4 cup lemon juice
(optional)

Lemon slices or fresh mint sprigs
(optional)

1 In a large pot bring the water to a rolling boil. Drop the tea bags into the water, cover, and remove from the heat. Allow the tea bags to steep for 60 minutes. (Steep for 45 minutes if you like a weaker tea.) After 60 minutes, remove the tea bags and add the sugar and optional lemon juice. Stir until the sugar completely dissolves.

2 Pour the tea into a pitcher and add ice cubes until the volume reaches 2 quarts. Serve over ice with lemon slices or fresh mint, if desired.

MAKES 2 QUARTS.

MEMA'S LEMON TEA

BERTHA DILLON (Crossville, Tennessee) is known as Mema to great-granddaughter **MASSEY PACK** (Nashville, Tennessee). Massey and her sister love to go and visit Mema because she's fun to play with and she always makes great food. Mema also lets Massey and sister Emmie play in the kitchen just like their mom, Ann, used to do.

I cup white grape juice

I gallon water

I ½ cups sugar

¾ cup lemonade mix powder

½ cup instant unsweetened iced tea powder

lemon slices or fresh mint sprigs (optional)

1 Pour the grape juice and water into a large pot. Add the sugar, lemonade mix, and instant tea. Stir until the sugar and powders dissolve.

2 Pour the tea into 2 different pitchers. Refrigerate until well chilled and serve over ice. Garnish with lemon slices or fresh mint, if desired.

MAKES 16 SERVINGS.

Nothing says summer to **NANCEE SHUTE** (Manchester, Tennessee) like fruit tea. She'd run to the house of her Grannie, **LOUISE WARNER** (Lexington, Kentucky), kiss her hello, and then head to Grannie's refrigerator. Nancee says, "She always had pitchers of some kind of cold, sweet, homemade fruit tea or lemonade. A couple of times my little brother and I begged to set up her beat-up card table for a makeshift stand and sell her sweet concoctions to neighbors outside. (In the fall we sold pumpkins a couple of times too.) We probably drank more than we sold, but it sure was fun. Grannie would come out and bring us a treat of something homemade while we sat out there with our jar of coins."

I 1/2 cups sugar

6 teaspoons instant unsweetened iced tea powder

12 cups water

I can (12 ounces) frozen lemonade, thawed

I can (12 ounces) frozen orange juice, thawed

lemon slices, orange slices, or fresh mint sprigs (optional)

---

1 Add the sugar, iced tea mix, and water to a large pot and mix until well dissolved. Add the thawed lemonade and orange juice and mix well.

2 Pour the tea into one 1-gallon container or two 2-quart pitchers. Refrigerate until well chilled and serve cold over ice. Garnish with lemon slices, orange slices, or fresh mint, if desired.

MAKES 16 SERVINGS.

MANDY HOLTSLDY BUTTERS (Brentwood, Tennessee) cherishes the handwritten recipes and letters that she has from MaMaw, **HELEN SPARKS NICHOLS** (Greenville, Kentucky). "While we only lived three hours away from her, she'd write me letters from the time I was little until I was much older," says Mandy. "As I little girl I was always so excited to get mail from her—as an adult, I'm so glad I saved those letters."

---

13 cups water, divided

4 small tea bags

2 cups sugar

juice of 3 medium lemons

I can (6 ounces) frozen orange juice, thawed

2 cups pineapple juice

---

1 In a saucepan bring 4 cups of the water to a boil. Turn off the heat. Steep the tea bags in the water for 3 minutes.

2 In a separate saucepan bring 3 cups of the water and the sugar to a boil.

3 In a large bowl or pitcher, combine the remaining 6 cups water with the lemon, orange, and pineapple juices. Mix well.

4 Combine all three mixtures and refrigerate until ready to serve. Heat the tea before serving.

MAKES 16 SERVINGS.

Cinnamon Rolls à la Mary (page 50)

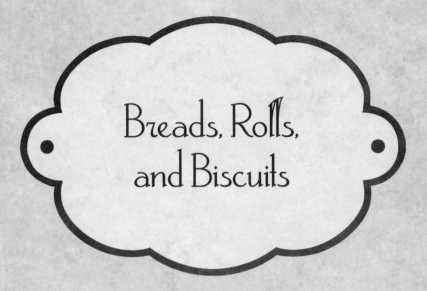

Breads, Rolls,
and Biscuits

Angel Biscuits
B. G.'s Hush Puppies
Cheese Biscuits
Hoecakes
Cinnamon Rolls à la Mary
Pumpkin Bread
Cranberry-Nut Bread
Momma Doye's Banana Bread
Braided Bread

ANGIE JONES (Thompson's Station, Tennessee) shares that she and her husband ate with Nanny, **BEATRICE SPAIN** (Nashville, Tennessee), and Papaw at least once a week during the first years of their marriage. Angie says, "We learned so much about how to love each other through the way they interacted in their kitchen. Her angel biscuits were my number one craving when I was pregnant with my first child. To this day, there is no better smell on earth."

1 envelope (.25 ounce) active dry yeast

2 tablespoons lukewarm water

5 cups all-purpose flour

1 teaspoon baking soda

3 teaspoons baking powder

1 teaspoon salt

1 cup shortening

2 cups buttermilk

1 Preheat the oven to 350 degrees.

2 In a small bowl dissolve the yeast in the lukewarm water. In a large bowl mix the flour, baking soda, baking powder, and salt. Cut the shortening into the flour mixture with a pastry cutter until the mixture is the texture of cornmeal. Make a well in the flour mixture. Add the yeast mixture and the buttermilk. Knead just enough for the dough to hold together.

3 On a well-floured work surface, roll out the dough to a $1/2$-inch thickness. Cut out the biscuits with a biscuit cutter or the rim of a glass. Place on an ungreased cookie sheet.

4 Bake for 20 minutes. Serve warm.

MAKES ABOUT 4 DOZEN BISCUITS.

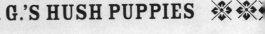

KATHERINE PAIGE HELTSLEY (Nashville, Tennessee) loves spending weekends in Camden, Tennessee, at her B. G.'s lake house. B. G. is **BETTY KEELING WOOTEN** (also of Nashville). B. G. bought Kate her very first fishing pole. Kate and her cousins fish at the lake house and love eating these hush puppies with step-granddad Big Jim's fried bass and catfish that the kids "helped" catch at the lake nearby.

---

2 cups self-rising cornmeal

2 tablespoons self-rising flour

½ medium onion, finely chopped

2 tablespoons finely chopped jalapeño peppers

1 cup buttermilk

1 large egg, beaten

vegetable oil for pan or deep-frying

---

1 In a large bowl combine the cornmeal, flour, onion, and jalapeños. Add the buttermilk and egg and mix well. Let the mixture stand for 5 to 7 minutes.

2 In a deep skillet or deep fryer, heat about 3 inches of oil over medium heat (to about 375 degrees). Drop the batter by tablespoons into the hot oil. Fry until golden brown, turning several times. Remove from the oil, drain, and blot well on paper towels before serving.

MAKES 4 TO 5 SERVINGS.

❈❈❈ CHEESE BISCUITS

SHIOKO MCGEE (Murfreesboro, Tennessee) is originally from Japan. She met her husband, Jeff, while he was in the military in Japan. Marrying into a Southern family, Shioko has heard about many of Jeff's favorites that his grandma, **ERMA SMITH** (Tupelo, Mississippi), made for him throughout his childhood. The family moved to Alaska when Jeff and his brother were in high school and they felt pretty far from the comforts of the South. Returning to Mississippi and their grandmother's house in the summer was the highlight of the year. They always enjoyed her biscuits, fried chicken, pies, and homemade candy. Her food was always worth the trip!

2 2/3 cups all-purpose flour	4 teaspoons baking powder	2/3 cup milk
I teaspoon salt	1/4 cup shortening	1/2 cup grated Cheddar cheese

1 Preheat the oven to 425 degrees.
2 Sift the flour, salt, and baking powder into a large bowl. Cut in the shortening until the flour mixture resembles coarse crumbs. Add the milk to make a soft dough.
3 Turn the dough out onto a lightly floured work surface and knead it gently. Roll the dough out to a 1/4-inch thickness. Sprinkle the cheese over the dough. Roll the dough up like a jelly roll and cut into 1/2-inch-thick slices. Place the biscuits cut side down on a greased cookie sheet.
4 Bake for about 15 minutes, until golden brown. Serve warm or cooled.

MAKES 2 DOZEN BISCUITS.

HOECAKES �֍ �֍ �֍

B. B. is what **Loran Gartner Johnson** (Hendersonville, Tennessee) calls her grandma, **Betty Keeling Wooten** (Nashville, Tennessee). Loran, her brother, and cousins love spending weekends in Camden, Tennessee, at B. B.'s lake house and eating these hoecakes with fried catfish caught at the nearby lake. Some parts of the country refer to these as johnnycakes. Hoecakes got their name because field hands often cooked these cakes on a shovel or a hoe held over a fire. Old-fashioned hoes were large and flat with a hole for the long handle to slide through. When making a hoecake, the blade was removed and placed over the fire to serve as the griddle.

2 cups cornmeal	2 cups boiling water	vegetable oil for frying
I teaspoon salt		

1 In a large bowl combine the cornmeal and the salt. Pour the boiling water over the cornmeal and stir it up. It will become a thick, stiff batter. Refrigerate for 30 minutes, or until well cooled.

2 Shape the batter into small oval patties.

3 Pour $1/2$ inch of oil in a large skillet and heat over medium-high heat. Place 4 to 5 patties at a time into the hot oil and fry. When the bottoms are brown, flip with tongs and cook the other side. When both sides are crispy and brown, transfer the patties to a plate, and drain well on layers of paper towel to remove the excess grease.

MAKES 4 TO 6 SERVINGS.

CINNAMON ROLLS À LA MARY

Author's note: I first met **MARY OETH** (Columbus, Georgia) during a college internship in Evansville, Indiana. We worked together at the Evansville Housing Authority and became friends. The last time we saw each other in person was in 1988, but we have kept in touch with cards each Christmas. Mary had baked me some of her breads to take home to my family for the holidays and had given me a few of her recipes way back then—she's an incredible baker. Recently I Googled her address and found a phone number, so I called her. We've since spoken a couple of times about this book. Who would have known when we first met that recipes would get us back in touch twenty-plus years later? Now Mary's back living in the South and I've made my home here as well. Mary is now eighty-five and a grandmother of three.

DOUGH:

2 cups water

1 tablespoon salt

1/2 cup plus 1 tablespoon sugar

3 tablespoons shortening

6 cups all-purpose flour

2 large eggs, beaten

3 envelopes (.25 ounce each) active dry yeast

1/3 cup lukewarm water

2 tablespoons butter, melted

FILLING:

1/4 cup sugar

1/4 cup ground cinnamon

1/2 cup chopped pecans or raisins (optional)

1 **TO MAKE THE DOUGH**, combine 2 cups water, salt, sugar, and shortening in a large saucepan and bring to a boil. Cool to lukewarm.

2 Add the flour and cooled liquid mixture to a large bowl. Mix until the mixture has the consistency of biscuit dough. Add the eggs and mix well. (More flour may be needed if the dough is too gooey.) In a small bowl crumble the yeast into 1/3 cup lukewarm water. Add the yeast mixture to the dough and mix well. Cover the dough and put it in the refrigerator to rise overnight.

3 Divide the dough in half. On a lightly floured work surface, roll out half of the dough to a $1/8$-inch thickness. Cover the top of the dough with the melted butter.

4 To **MAKE THE FILLING**, mix the sugar and cinnamon. Sprinkle the dough well with the sugar and cinnamon mixture. Sprinkle with half of the pecans or raisins, if desired.

5 Roll up the dough like a jelly roll and cut it into 1-inch slices. Place the slices cut side down on a greased cookie sheet. Sprinkle lightly with remaining cinnamon and sugar. Repeat with the other dough half. Let the slices rise until they double in size, approximately 2 hours.

6 Preheat the oven to 350 degrees. Bake until brown, 10 to 15 minutes. Serve warm.

MAKES 18 ROLLS.

✦✦✦ PUMPKIN BREAD

HEIDI NICHOLS (Hermitage, Tennessee) loves the holidays with her Nana, **SARAH LANCASTER** (Lexington, Kentucky). Heidi says, "From as far back as I can remember, she has made every holiday special—even the 'smaller' ones. Of course, Christmas, Thanksgiving, and Easter were big, but she'd also make us cookies or special treats for Valentine's Day, July 4th, and Halloween. This pumpkin bread is a favorite of mine from her 'fall collection.'"

I 1/2 cups sugar

1/4 teaspoon baking powder

I teaspoon baking soda

3/4 teaspoon salt

2 large eggs

I teaspoon ground cloves

I teaspoon ground nutmeg

I 2/3 cups all-purpose flour

1/2 cup vegetable oil

1/2 cup water

I cup canned pumpkin

1/2 cup chopped pecans

---

1 Preheat the oven to 350 degrees.

2 In a large bowl combine the sugar, baking powder, baking soda, salt, eggs, cloves, nutmeg, flour, oil, water, pumpkin, and pecans, mixing well after each addition. Pour the batter into a greased and floured 9 x 5-inch loaf pan.

3 Bake for I hour and 15 minutes, or until a toothpick inserted in the center comes out clean. Allow to cool on a wire rack for at least 30 minutes before slicing. Serve warm or at room temperature.

MAKES 1 LOAF.

CRANBERRY-NUT BREAD

Katie Braman (Nashville, Tennessee) shares that her Mimi, **Rudell Blalock**, was born and raised in Sedalia, Kentucky, and now lives in Paducah, Kentucky. "Mimi, her mom, and my mom are all great cooks and bakers," Katie adds. "Mimi is well-known for this incredible cranberry bread."

- 2 cups all-purpose flour
- 1 cup sugar
- 1/2 teaspoon baking powder
- 1 teaspoon salt
- 1/2 teaspoon baking soda
- 3/4 cup orange juice
- 2 tablespoons vegetable oil
- 1 tablespoon grated orange rind
- 1 large egg, well beaten
- 1/2 cup fresh or frozen cranberries, halved
- 1/2 cup chopped walnuts

1. Preheat the oven to 350 degrees.
2. In a medium bowl mix the flour, sugar, baking powder, salt, and baking soda. Stir in the orange juice, oil, orange rind, and egg. Stir until well blended. Mix in the cranberries and walnuts. Pour the batter into a greased 9 x 5-inch loaf pan.
3. Bake for 55 minutes, or until a toothpick inserted in the center comes out clean. Cool in the pan on a wire rack for 15 minutes, and then remove the bread from the pan.

MAKES 1 LOAF.

MOMMA DOYE'S BANANA BREAD

Momma Doye is what **LIBBY LEVERETT-CREW** (Nashville, Tennessee) called her grand-mother, **DOYE BROWN VANDIVER JOHNSON** (Burns, Tennessee). "Momma Doye always said that if you tasted the food while you were cooking, it made it that much sweeter," Libby recalls. "She had a little stool that she kept in the kitchen so I could help her cook and do dishes. She also made me a child's apron, which I still have and my daughter used when she was little. She taught me how to whip potatoes and roll out pastry for fruit pies before I was knee-high to a grasshopper. While I spent a lot of time cooking my entire life, there are still some recipes that I cannot replicate—no matter how closely I follow them. I do think I have the whipped potatoes down, but my roasts, biscuits, cornbread, or green beans are never like hers. Maybe I don't taste them enough during preparation!"

---

4 medium-size ripe
   bananas, mashed

2 cups sugar

2 large eggs

I cup melted
   margarine

I cup buttermilk

I teaspoon baking
   soda

I teaspoon baking
   powder

pinch of salt

2 ½ cups all-purpose
   flour

I teaspoon vanilla
   extract

---

1 Preheat the oven to 350 degrees.

2 In a large bowl cream together the bananas and sugar. Add the eggs and beat well. Add the melted margarine, buttermilk, baking soda, baking powder, salt, flour, and vanilla and mix well. Pour the batter into a lightly greased 9 x 5-inch loaf pan.

3 Bake for 30 to 40 minutes, or until a toothpick inserted into the center comes out clean. Let the bread cool in the pan for 10 minutes, and then transfer to a wire rack to finish cooling before slicing.

MAKES 1 LOAF.

MARY OETH (Columbus, Georgia) was born in a small town near Waverly, Tennessee. She loved being outdoors and followed her dad around like a puppy dog, she shares. "When I was a young girl, I was more interested in being with my dad—I was a tomboy." At 85, she's a proud great-great grandma. Her family now includes four great-great grandsons, six great grandchildren, and three granddaughters. Her niece's ten-year-old son wants to be a chef. "He recently came by to visit and I gave him some of my recipes and told him to take any of my books that he wanted," Mary shares.

1/2 cup sugar	4 large eggs, divided	I cup lukewarm water
1/2 cup shortening	2 envelopes (.25 ounce each) active dry yeast	6 1/2 cups all-purpose flour, divided
2 teaspoons salt		
I cup hot milk		

---

1 Place the sugar, shortening, and salt in large bowl. Add the hot milk, stir to soften the shortening, and then cool. Beat in 2 of the eggs. In a small bowl dissolve the yeast in the lukewarm water. Stir the yeast mixture into the shortening mixture. Add 4 cups of the flour and beat until smooth. Add enough of the remaining flour to make a soft dough.

2 Turn the dough out on a floured work surface and knead it by hand until smooth, 8 to 10 minutes. Place the dough in a greased bowl, turning once to grease the surface of the dough. Cover the dough with a dish towel and let it rise in a warm place until it doubles in size, about 1 hour and 15 minutes. Punch the dough down and let it rest for 10 minutes.

3 Divide the dough into 6 pieces. Roll each into a rope 15 inches long. Place the ropes on a greased cookie sheet and shape into 2 braids, using 3 ropes for each. Let the braided dough rise until it doubles in size, 45 to 60 minutes.

4 Brush the tops of the loaves with the whites from the remaining 2 eggs—do not beat the egg whites.

5 Preheat the oven to 375 degrees. Bake for 20 to 25 minutes.

MAKES 2 BRAIDED LOAVES.

Chicken Soup with Homemade Noodles (page 74)

Appetizers,
Soups, and Salads

Cucumber Sandwiches

Pimento Cheese à la Nanny

Artichoke Seafood Dip

Meme's Mushrooms

Pecan Cheese Ball

Sausage Balls

Ham and Cheese Party Spread

Steak Soup

Supper Corn Chowder

D-Dot's Kale Soup

Chicken Soup with Homemade
Noodles

Soup Beans and Skillet
Cornbread

Stuffed Potato Soup

Vegetable Soup

Southern-Style Chili

Cranberry Salad

Mamaw's Tuna Salad

MeMaw's Corn 'n' "Cucs"

Broccoli Salad

Granny's Potato Salad

Seven-Layer Salad

Wise and Otherwise Apricot
Salad

Nanny's Bridal Salad

Three-Bean Salad

Sawdust Salad

Sweet Slaw

Beet Salad

CUCUMBER SANDWICHES

NINA FERGUSON (Louisville, Kentucky) shares that her Grandmother Frankie, **FRANCES LANE** (White House, Tennessee), taught all of her five girls to cook. As young girls, Nina and her close-in-age cousin Debby loved to play together and be around Frankie and all of their aunts when they were cooking together. They felt like little princesses when they got to have these "fancy" finger sandwiches while waiting for the big meal.

1 package (8 ounces) cream cheese, softened

3 medium cucumbers, peeled

3 medium green onions

1/4 teaspoon Worcestershire sauce

1/4 teaspoon seasoned salt

16 slices sandwich bread

1 Beat the cream cheese in the bowl of an electric mixer until smooth and creamy.
2 Cut the cucumbers in half lengthwise and discard the seeds. Process the cucumbers in a food processor until they are finely chopped. Drain the cucumbers and press dry. Process the green onions until finely chopped.
3 Add the cucumbers, green onions, Worcestershire sauce, and seasoned salt to the cream cheese mixture. Mix well.
4 Trim the crusts from the bread. Spread the cucumber mixture on half of the bread slices and top with the remaining slices. Tightly wrap the sandwiches in plastic wrap and chill until firm, about 60 minutes. When ready to serve, cut each sandwich into 4 triangles and arrange on a serving plate.

MAKES 32 TRIANGLES.

PIMENTO CHEESE À LA NANNY

REBECCA BARBER (Smyrna, Tennessee) remembers that her Nanny, **EVELYN BARBER** (Nashville, Tennessee), would make this pimento cheese a lot during the summer and it was always a big hit. "Nanny loved to cook and bake and felt all ladies needed to know how," Rebecca says. "As soon as we were old enough, she let us help in the kitchen and was very patient trying to show us what to do. It was great helping her because she made it fun and we had some of our best talks cooking in the kitchen."

1 pound sharp
    Cheddar cheese

½ pound Monterey
    Jack cheese

2 medium kosher dill
    pickles

2 cloves garlic

3 heaping
    tablespoons
    mayonnaise

I jar (4 ounces)
    pimientos, drained

1 Cut the Cheddar cheese, Monterey Jack cheese, pickles, and garlic into large chunks. Place the chunks in a food processor. Process until the garlic and pickles are broken down, but do not puree the mixture.

2 Transfer the mixture to a large bowl, add the mayonnaise and pimientos, and mix well. Cover and refrigerate for at least 2 hours before serving. To serve as an appetizer, spread on bread, crackers, or celery.

MAKES 8 SERVINGS.

ARTICHOKE SEAFOOD DIP

KATHERINE PAIGE HELTSLEY (Hendersonville, Tennessee) was the first girl to come along in two generations. Her grandmother, Jules, **JULIE EATON HELTSLEY** (Tullahoma, Tennessee), had raised three boys, so she was excited to do "girlie" things. When Kate was born, Jules bought a tea set that sits on a little table in the corner of her dining room. She leaves it out so she's always available for a tea party when Kate visits. Jules is known far and wide for her cooking and she's also a great seamstress. She made Easter outfits and smocked dresses for Kate the first few years of her life. And Kate still loves sleeping with the Winnie the Pooh quilt that Jules made for her as a baby.

I can (14 ounces) artichoke hearts, drained and chopped

I cup mayonnaise

I cup grated Parmesan cheese

I package (6 ounces) frozen crab, thawed, drained, and flaked

2 tablespoons dry seasoned bread crumbs

I tablespoon finely chopped fresh parsley

---

1 In a medium bowl combine the artichoke hearts, mayonnaise, cheese, and crab. Spoon the mixture into a lightly greased, microwave-safe I-quart casserole dish.

2 Microwave on medium for 30 seconds. Stir well. Stirring every I 1/2 minutes, microwave on medium for another 6 to 7 minutes, until heated through.

3 Combine the bread crumbs and parsley in a small bowl and sprinkle on top of the dip. Microwave on medium for another 30 to 45 seconds, or brown in the oven. Serve the dip hot with crackers.

MAKES 2 TO 3 CUPS.

❖❖❖ MEME'S MUSHROOMS

Meme **DOROTHY GREEN** was born in Florida and later lived in Nashville, Tennessee. Granddaughter **SHAY ASHCRAFT** (also of Nashville) says Meme's stuffed mushrooms were a favorite at Thanksgiving and Christmas. She also recalls, "My aunt and little brother loved the stuffing so much, but they refused to eat the mushroom caps. So Meme would double the recipe so that Aunt Kathy and Kyle could eat the stuffing directly out of the bowl—she'd use the rest to stuff the mushroom caps for the rest of the family."

12 fresh mushrooms (caps the size of half-dollars)

3 slices bacon

1/3 cup finely chopped green onions

1/2 teaspoon salt

1/4 teaspoon black pepper

3 drops hot sauce

1 tablespoon all-purpose flour

1/4 cup heavy whipping cream

2 tablespoons shredded Cheddar cheese

1 Wash the mushrooms well. Carefully remove the caps and set aside. Finely chop the mushroom stems. Place the mushroom caps on a paper towel on a dinner plate. Microwave for 1 minute and drain.

2 Fry the bacon in a saucepan for 2 1/2 to 3 minutes, or until crisp. Blot off the excess grease, crumble the bacon, and put it back in the skillet. Add the chopped mushroom stems, green onions, salt, pepper, and hot sauce. Sauté until the mushrooms and onions are tender. Blend in the flour and then stir in the cream until smooth. Heat on low until thickened and creamy, stirring once or twice during cooking. Stir in the cheese and remove from the heat.

3 Fill each mushroom cap with the skillet mixture and place around the outer edge of a microwave-safe plate. Before serving, microwave 1 minute, or until heated through.

MAKES 1 DOZEN MUSHROOMS.

PECAN CHEESE BALL

PAM DIXON (Hermitage, Tennessee) loved any chance she got to go to her Mimi's house. Mimi, **STELLA MOORE** (Columbia, Tennessee), always had "special snacks" to eat, even when she was making a big meal. You'd never catch her "opening a bag" of anything—she always took care to make us great food and snacks. I always felt like I could taste her love in every bite!

I pound bacon

4 cups shredded Cheddar cheese

2 packages (8 ounces each) cream cheese

I pound pecans, chopped

3 teaspoons minced garlic

3 tablespoons paprika

3 tablespoons chili powder

1 Fry the bacon in a skillet, drain off the grease, and crumble the bacon.

2 Place the bacon in a large bowl and add the Cheddar cheese, cream cheese, pecans, and garlic. Mix well.

3 Divide the mixture in half and shape each half into a ball. On a large piece of wax paper, sprinkle the paprika and chili powder. Place one of the cheese balls on the wax paper and roll it through the spice mixture. Do the same with the other cheese ball. Wrap each ball in wax paper and refrigerate for at least 6 hours before serving.

MAKES 2 CHEESE BALLS.

SAUSAGE BALLS ❈❈❈

MABEL HIGGINS (Old Hickory, Tennessee) shares that when you sat down to eat at Papaw and Mamaw's house, she would keep putting food on the table until the table was near full. Mabel recalls, "You'd have to keep saying, 'Mamaw, that's enough. Come sit down!' She would just keep the food coming if you didn't try to stop her." Mamaw was **MARGARET HIPPS RICKER** (Greeneville, Tennessee).

---

1 pound ground sausage (mild, medium, or hot)

3 cups Bisquick

2 cups shredded sharp Cheddar cheese

2 tablespoons milk

---

1 Preheat the oven to 350 degrees.

2 Brown the sausage in a skillet and drain off the grease.

3 In a large bowl combine the sausage, Bisquick, cheese, and milk. Mix until all the ingredients are well combined.

4 Roll the mixture into small balls and place on a cookie sheet.

5 Bake for 15 to 18 minutes, until well browned.

MAKES 3 DOZEN SAUSAGE BALLS

HAM AND CHEESE PARTY SPREAD

There was nothing like a tea party under one of the old willow trees on a cool fall day with her Grannie, **LOUISE WARNER** (Lexington, Kentucky), recalls granddaughter **NANCEE SHUTE** (Manchester, Tennessee). Nancee says, "Grannie would make hot tea and put it in a thermos—I think it tasted better coming out of there! And she'd always have a plate of something special to go with it. We'd sit out under that tree and sip tea and eat crackers or little bread sandwiches with homemade spread. How I long for an afternoon like that once more."

---

1 package (6 ounces) thinly sliced ham, diced

3 medium green onions, finely chopped

1 package (8 ounces) cream cheese, softened

1 1/2 teaspoons Worcestershire sauce

1 tablespoon mayonnaise

---

1 Combine the ham, green onions, cream cheese, Worcestershire sauce, and mayonnaise in a medium bowl until well blended.

2 Place the spread in a small serving dish and refrigerate for at least 4 hours. Serve on crackers or bread squares.

MAKES 10 TO 12 SERVINGS.

STEAK SOUP

SARAH LANGSTON (Saltillo, Mississippi) was known to her grandchildren as Mammy, shares NANCY SMITH McGEE (Murfreesboro, Tennessee). Mammy's family was especially poor, as most farmers were back in the day. "Chicken and pork were staple foods, as the cows typically brought more money when they were sold to slaughter," Sarah says. "Occasionally someone would give Mammy several pounds of beef, which she used to make steak soup—the beef would go farther in soup than it would prepared in other ways. Mammy would always say, 'Don't waste your food. There are less fortunate people than us who don't have anything.'"

I stick butter

I cup all-purpose flour

2 quarts water

I pound ground beef

I cup diced onions

I cup sliced carrots

I can (14.75 ounces) creamed corn

I cup chopped potatoes

I cup parboiled lima beans

I can (12 ounces) tomato juice

I tablespoon seasoned salt

9 beef bouillon cubes

I teaspoon black pepper

1 In a large pot or Dutch oven, melt the butter and gradually stir in the flour. Add the water.

2 In a large skillet, sauté the ground beef until cooked through. Rinse the beef and drain well.

3 Add the beef to the soup mixture. Add the onions, carrots, creamed corn, potatoes, lima beans, tomato juice, seasoned salt, bouillon cubes, and black pepper and bring to a boil. Reduce the heat and simmer for 45 to 55 minutes, until all the vegetables are tender. Do not add salt. Serve hot.

MAKES 6 SERVINGS.

❖❖❖ SUPPER CORN CHOWDER

While Nana, **Anita Sherrill**, lives in Peachtree City, Georgia, she was born and raised in Hattiesburg, Mississippi. Her granddaughter, **Bethany Mason** (Nashville, Tennessee), shares that this corn chowder is a favorite of her father's. Bethany says, "My sister and I have memories of Nana in the kitchen working with items from her garden—corn, blueberries, squash, green beans—she is a wonderful cook!" Although Nana doesn't get around very well anymore, she still insists on getting in the kitchen. One of my favorite things to hear her say is, "It ain't a dessert unless it has Cool Whip on top."

---

4 large Yukon gold
potatoes, peeled
and diced

6 slices bacon

2 medium onions,
sliced in rings

1 cup fresh whole-
kernel corn
(grilled is best)

1 can (10.75 ounces)
cream of
mushroom soup

3 cups milk

1/4 teaspoon salt

1/4 teaspoon black
pepper

6 fresh thyme sprigs

---

1 Boil the potatoes in a large pot until tender.

2 While the potatoes are cooking, in a large skillet fry the bacon until crisp. Remove the bacon, pour off the drippings, and return about 3 tablespoons of the grease to the skillet. Crumble the bacon and set it aside.

3 Add the onions to the skillet and cook until lightly browned. Drain the potatoes and return to the large pot. Add the onions, corn, soup, milk, salt, pepper, and thyme sprigs. Heat to boiling, then reduce the heat and simmer for at least 10 minutes before serving. Remove the thyme sprigs, ladle into bowls, and top each serving with the crumbled bacon.

MAKES 6 SERVINGS.

ALLI CREW (Nashville, Tennessee) calls her grandma D-Dot. D-Dot, **DOT VANDIVER LEVERETT** (Goodlettsville, Tennessee), always says "hidee" when she calls. Alli says, "At Christmas, D-Dot, my mother, and I make holiday goodies together. We make peanut butter balls, rum balls, Cap'n Crunch drops, pretzels dipped in chocolate, fudge, penuche, peanut brittle, cookies, and so many other yummy treats. We make huge batches of each and package them in festive containers to give to our loved ones. While we're cooking and baking, we dance, sing, tell stories, and laugh—a lot!"

2 bunches kale

1 pound ground beef

1 ½ pounds kielbasa, sliced

1 medium onion, chopped

1 teaspoon salt

10 cups water

1 can (16 ounces) kidney beans, drained

1 small head cabbage, chopped

6 large potatoes, peeled and cubed

1 Thoroughly wash the kale. Cut off the stems and slice into small strips.

2 Add the ground beef, kielbasa, onion, salt, and water to a large Dutch oven and bring to a boil. Reduce to medium heat and simmer until the ground beef is cooked through.

3 Add the kale, beans, and cabbage and simmer until the kale is about half-done, 20 to 30 minutes. Add the potatoes and cook at a low boil for 30 minutes, or until the potatoes are tender. Serve the soup with warm, crusty bread, if desired.

MAKES 6 TO 8 SERVINGS.

CHICKEN SOUP WITH HOMEMADE NOODLES

DEBBY WHITE (White House, Tennessee) shares that her Grandmother Frankie, **FRANCES LANE** (also of White House), made her dumplings and noodles from scratch. Debby says, "One Thanksgiving, Grandmother's sister introduced what was, for its time, a wonderful new and miraculous kitchen helper: a pressure cooker. While Grandmother's noodles were cooking, my mother couldn't contain herself, so she decided to take a peek. She opened the top of the new pressure cooker without allowing the pressure to escape. As you can imagine, it was an instantaneous atomic explosion of noodles! Hot noodles, hot broth, loud screams, and then cries due to the loss of noodles! Initially, no one seemed to care about burns from volcanic broth and the noodles that were hotter than firecrackers. While Grandmother, Aunt Hallie, and my mother have passed on, the 'noodle explosion story' will live forever!"

NOODLES:
- 1 cup all-purpose flour
- 1/4 teaspoon salt
- 2 tablespoons water
- 1 large egg, beaten

SOUP:
- 1 chicken (3 pounds), cut up
- 1/2 cup chopped onion, divided
- 2 chicken bouillon cubes
- 1 bay leaf
- 1/4 teaspoon black pepper
- 1/2 cup sliced celery
- 2 large carrots, thinly sliced

---

1 **TO MAKE THE NOODLES**, mix the flour and salt in a small bowl, making a well in the center. Add the water and egg. Using your fingers, form the dough. Wrap the dough in plastic wrap and let it sit for 60 minutes.

2 **TO MAKE THE SOUP**, rinse the raw chicken well. In a large pot or Dutch oven, combine the chicken with 1/4 cup of the onions, the bouillon cubes, bay leaf, pepper, and enough hot water to cover. Bring to a boil and then reduce the heat. Cover and simmer cover for 45 minutes, or until the chicken is tender.

3 Remove the chicken and chop it into bite-size pieces, discarding the skin and bones. Skim any grease off the top of the broth and add enough water to measure 7 to 8 cups. Add the chicken pieces, celery, carrots, and remaining $1/4$ cup onion. Bring to a boil. Cook over medium heat for 10 minutes or until the carrots are crisp-tender. Remove the bay leaf.

4 To finish the noodles, roll out the dough as thin as possible on a floured work surface. Fold it loosely into thirds and then cut into $1/2$-inch slices. Unfold the dough and cut on the former fold lines. Drop the dough into the simmering soup. Simmer for another 5 to 10 minutes or until the noodles are tender.

MAKES 10 SERVINGS.

❄ SOUP BEANS AND SKILLET CORNBREAD

Soup beans and cornbread are a staple and a much-loved comfort food in Appalachian Virginia. MICHELLE FLEMING (Nashville, Tennessee) said that her Granny, HAZEL VIVIAN YATES FLEMING (Clintwood, Virginia), made the best and thinking of it brings back warm memories. "Granny was big on hugs, laughter, Jesus, her garden, and feeding her immediate and extended family and friends," Michelle recalls. "Granny would shoo my cousins and me away from the stove, but we'd sit at her big kitchen table and drink gallons of Kool-Aid while she cooked, laughed, and talked to us. I lost her way too early—1976. I miss her in new ways as I grow older. She loved us all unconditionally and taught me about forgiveness and grace."

SOUP:

1 package (1 pound) dried pinto beans

1/2 teaspoon salt, divided

1 ham hock

5 1/2 cups water

1/2 teaspoon black pepper

4 slices hickory-smoked bacon

CORNBREAD:

6 slices thick bacon (save grease)

2 cups self-rising cornmeal

2 tablespoons all-purpose flour

1 large egg

1 cup buttermilk

1/2 cup water

---

1 **TO MAKE THE SOUP**, soak the beans overnight in water and 1/4 teaspoon of the salt. Drain the beans and rinse with cold water.

2 Place the beans and ham hock in a large pot and cover with 5 1/2 cups water. Bring to a low boil, stir, reduce the heat to low, and cover. Cook for about 2 hours, stirring frequently. Make sure the beans stay covered with water. Add the remaining 1/4 teaspoon salt and the pepper to season as you cook.

3 Fry the bacon until done and save the drippings. Crumble the bacon and add to the soup mixture, along with the drippings. Cook an additional 60 minutes over low heat, stirring frequently.

4 **To make the cornbread**, preheat the oven to 450 degrees. Fry the bacon in a cast-iron skillet. Keep the grease warm in the skillet after frying the bacon. Set the bacon aside for another use. Place the cornmeal, flour, egg, buttermilk, water, and half of the bacon grease in a large bowl and stir until the mixture is the consistency of cake batter. Add more water, if needed. You just want enough grease left in the skillet to coat the bottom and sides; if you have too much pour the extra out.

5 Pour the batter into the skillet. Place the skillet in the oven and bake for 30 minutes, checking often. Remove from the oven and slice immediately.

6 When ready to eat, ladle the soup into individual bowls. Crumble a slice of hot cornbread into each bowl, mix, and serve.

MAKES 6 TO 8 SERVINGS.

Tip: *If your cast-iron skillet is fairly new and not well cured yet, add a few drops of oil (any kind) to coat it before adding bacon.*

STUFFED POTATO SOUP

JENNY LEWIS (Nashville, Tennessee) shares that her mother inherited her mother's ability to cook and bake. While Jenny and her mom baked all kinds of pies at Thanksgiving and Christmas, Jenny's mom would relate stories of Grandma Wolfe, **NORA VIRGINIA WOLFE HOULDERSHELL** (Moorefield, West Virginia), and how she dried fruit (with clothespins on a clothesline on the porch) and never threw anything away. "They used everything for baking or cooking," Jenny says. "They called the dried apple peels 'apple snits' and hung them on the tree at Christmas along with popcorn, cranberries, and other edibles. Grandma Wolfe made watermelon wine from the flesh and juice, pickles from the rind, and planted the seeds—she made good use of everything! They had a root cellar (a hole dug in the ground) where they kept potatoes, onions, and other veggies they were storing so they could dig them up and eat them all winter. My grandma was organic and 'green' before it was ever thought of!"

4 cups water, divided

4 chicken bouillon cubes

1/4 cup chopped onion

1 cup milk

2 cans (10.75 ounces each) cream of chicken soup

1/8 teaspoon garlic powder

1/8 teaspoon onion salt

6 cups cubed potatoes

1 pound Velveeta cheese, cubed

Sliced green onion tops (optional)

Crumbled bacon (optional)

1 In a large pot or Dutch oven, combine 1 cup of the water, the bouillon cubes, and the onion and simmer for 30 minutes.

2 In a large saucepan combine the remaining 3 cups water, the milk, cream of chicken soup, garlic powder, and onion salt. Cook over low heat until the soup is creamy and any lumps have been stirred out.

3 Pour the soup mixture into the Dutch oven with the bouillon and onion mixture. Add the potatoes and cook over medium heat. When the potatoes are almost done, add the cheese. Remove from the heat so the cheese won't stick. Once the cheese has substantially melted, return the pot to low heat and simmer until you are ready to serve. Top with sliced green onion tops or bacon, if desired.

MAKES 6 TO 8 SERVINGS.

❖❖ VEGETABLE SOUP

JO McCLOUD (Chattanooga, Tennessee) says that her Granny, LOUISE HOLLIS (also of Chattanooga), lived with her family and watched her and her three brothers while their parents worked. Granny was a funny lady, with many great quotes and sayings, so she kept them all in stitches. Jo says she learned how to cook from Granny as well.

I tablespoon vegetable oil

1/2 cup diced carrots

1/2 cup diced celery

1/2 cup chopped white or yellow onion

1/2 teaspoon minced garlic

3 cups water

2 cups chicken or beef broth

1/2 cup chopped yellow summer squash

1/2 cup chopped zucchini

I can (14.5 ounces) diced tomatoes

I large white potato, peeled and cubed

I can (16 ounces) great Northern beans, drained

1/2 teaspoon salt

1/4 teaspoon black pepper

1 Pour the oil into a large pot or Dutch oven. Add the carrots, celery, onion, and garlic and sauté over medium heat until tender.

2 Add the water, broth, yellow squash, zucchini, tomatoes, potato, and beans. Bring to a boil, reduce the heat, and simmer uncovered for 35 to 40 minutes. Add the salt and pepper, stir, and serve hot.

MAKES 6 SERVINGS.

SOUTHERN-STYLE CHILI

JENN LAWSON (Mobile, Alabama) shares that her dad's mom, GERTIE VIOLA LAWSON (Nashville, Tennessee), was a large woman who gave the best hugs. "When there's a chill in the air, I think of her and the chili and soups she used to make for us," Jenn says. "We'd dip our grilled cheese or cornbread in the broth. Gran Gert always had on lipstick and she wore Avon perfume. Avon used to make collectible bottles for some of their women's and men's fragrances, and she kept the empties when she and granddad would finish them. I remember bottles shaped like a turtle, an old car, and a bowling pin—I liked to rearrange them on her on her dressing table."

4 pounds ground beef

1 large onion, finely chopped

1 large green bell pepper, finely chopped

2 teaspoons garlic powder

3 tablespoons chili powder

1 tablespoon paprika

1 tablespoon crushed red pepper flakes

1 teaspoon dried thyme

1 teaspoon salt

2 teaspoons black pepper

1 celery stalk, finely chopped

2 cans (28 ounces each) diced tomatoes

2 cans (28 ounces each) tomato puree

2 cans (8 ounces each) tomato sauce

3 cans (16 ounces each) kidney beans, drained

1 can (16 ounces) kidney beans, drained and pureed

1 In a large pot or Dutch oven, brown the ground beef with the onion, green pepper, garlic powder, chili powder, paprika, red pepper flakes, thyme, salt, and black pepper. Stir frequently and drain off any grease.

2 Add the celery, diced tomatoes, tomato puree, tomato sauce, whole beans, and pureed beans and mix well. Simmer for 60 minutes. Serve hot. This soup goes well with cornbread.

MAKES 20 SERVINGS.

CRANBERRY SALAD

Grandmother **RUBY BROYLES** was born in Port Arthur, Texas, and lived in Nederland, Texas, until she passed away. **BETHANY MASON** (Nashville, Tennessee) says her cranberry salad was also affectionately known as "red stuff." It was a wonderful addition to turkey dinners and was a traditional staple at their Thanksgiving meal for as long as she can remember.

2 large apples, peeled, cored, and chopped

I package (12 ounces) fresh cranberries

I ½ cups sugar

I cup chopped pecans

I container (8 ounces) frozen whipped topping, thawed

I cup miniature marshmallows

1 Add the apples, cranberries, and sugar to a food processor and process. Cover and refrigerate for 60 minutes.

2 Pour the fruit mixture into a medium bowl. Add the pecans, whipped topping, and marshmallows and mix together. Cover and refrigerate until serving. The salad can also be frozen.

MAKES 4 TO 6 SERVINGS.

MAMAW'S TUNA SALAD

"My Mamaw, **KELLY BLEWSTER** (Magnolia, Arkansas), was an excellent cook," shares **JAMEY KELLY BLEWSTER SIMS** (Springdale, Arkansas). Jamey says, "When she and my papaw built their house in Magnolia, Arkansas, she was somewhat of a pioneer. With the readily accessible *Kitchen Designs* magazine and her local do-it-yourself store, she designed her own kitchen." That house is now a physician's office and on a recent visit to her childhood home, my mom talked to a nurse who works there. The nurse said employees think the house is haunted—lights flicker and strange noises are heard. "It's not haunted, but there is a ghost in there—it's my mother, and she's in the kitchen cooking," my mother answered with a giggle.

- 2 cans (6 ounces each) tuna
- 4 large eggs, hard-boiled and finely chopped
- 1 jar (4 ounces) pimientos
- 1/2 cup mayonnaise
- 1 cup chopped celery
- 1 teaspoon lemon pepper seasoning
- 1/2 teaspoon black pepper
- 1 can (14.75 ounces) corn, drained
- 1/2 cup chopped red or green bell pepper
- 1/2 teaspoon McCormick Salad Supreme seasoning

1 Rinse and drain the tuna and flake into a medium bowl.

2 Add the eggs, pimientos and liquid, mayonnaise, celery, lemon pepper seasoning, black pepper, corn, bell pepper, and Salad Supreme seasoning. Cover and refrigerate for 2 hours before serving. If desired, serve on lettuce with crackers or cucumber or bell pepper strips.

MAKES 4 TO 6 SERVINGS.

MEMAW'S CORN 'N' "CUCS"

LOUISE JOHNSON (Nashville, Tennessee) shares that her MeMaw, **FRAN OLNEY** (Paducah, Kentucky), could always make her laugh. "She was a strong, tall woman who always had a smile on her face like she was up to something," says Louise. "She shortened words and had some great one-liners like 'Well, shuck my corn!' And she always called her home-grown cucumbers 'cucs.'"

I cup frozen corn

2 medium cucumbers, peeled and thinly sliced

1/2 medium onion, thinly sliced

1/2 cup distilled white vinegar

2 tablespoons sugar

2 tablespoons water

I teaspoon dill

1/2 teaspoon parsley

1/8 teaspoon salt

1/4 teaspoon black pepper

---

1 Prepare the corn according to the package directions. Drain the corn.

2 Place the cucumbers and onion in a large bowl and add the corn.

3 In a small bowl combine the vinegar, sugar, water, dill, parsley, salt, and pepper and blend well.

4 Pour the dressing over the vegetables and mix well. Cover and refrigerate for at least 2 hours. Toss before serving.

MAKES 6 SERVINGS.

❧❧❧ BROCCOLI SALAD

Although surprising in the South, fresh and healthy was the way her mom, **KAREN SUE GREGG WILLHOIT** (Falmouth, Virginia), always cooked, shares **LEIGH WILLHOIT DOUCET** (Ruther Glen, Virginia). "I've got daughters of my own now and do the same for them," says Leigh. "Their grandmother lost her battle to breast cancer in 2001. While they will never know her personally, I hope to impart to them so much of what she taught me."

8 slices bacon

2 heads broccoli, cut into small florets

1/2 cup raisins

1/4 cup chopped red onion

1 1/4 cups mayonnaise

1/4 cup sugar

1/8 cup red wine vinegar

1/4 cup finely chopped almonds or walnuts (optional)

1 Place the bacon in a skillet and cook over medium heat until done. Drain, blot on paper towels, and crumble.

2 Combine the broccoli, bacon, raisins, and onion in a medium bowl.

3 In small bowl combine the mayonnaise, sugar, and vinegar until well blended.

4 Cover and refrigerate both bowls for 2 hours. Before serving, pour the mayonnaise mixture over the broccoli mixture and toss. If adding nuts, stir in right before serving.

MAKES 6 TO 8 SERVINGS.

GRANNY'S POTATO SALAD

This recipe doesn't sound fancy, and really it isn't. But according to **AMY DEDRICK PETERSON** (Mobile, Alabama), her Granny's potato salad was a highly coveted side dish at every family event. Granny, **ALICE MAY DOWNEY** (also of Mobile), always made Amy her own bowl of potato salad. Amy recalls, "She would hide it until everyone else left and give it to me. No one ever knew she was sneaking me more of her coveted potato salad until I moved back to Mobile after college. If she just made it and it wasn't for a special occasion, she'd call me to come get some or drop it by my house. It probably wasn't a big deal to everyone else, but it was a very special memory (and really good secret) between me and my Granny."

---

5 large red potatoes, cut into large chunks

3 large eggs, hard-boiled, divided

I teaspoon dry mustard

2 tablespoons Hellmann's Sandwich Spread

3 tablespoons mayonnaise

1/4 teaspoon salt

1/2 teaspoon black pepper

3 tablespoons sweet pickle relish

1/2 teaspoon parsley

1/4 teaspoon paprika

---

1 Boil the potatoes in a large pot of water until tender. Let the potatoes cool. Once cool, peel and chop the potatoes into cubes.

2 Dice 2 of the eggs.

3 In a medium bowl mix the potatoes, diced eggs, mustard, sandwich spread, mayonnaise, salt, pepper, and relish.

4 Slice the remaining egg and place it on top of the salad. Sprinkle the parsley and then the paprika on top. Cover and refrigerate for 2 to 3 hours before serving.

MAKES 6 TO 8 SERVINGS.

SEVEN-LAYER SALAD

MADELINE REYNOLDS (Nashville, Tennessee) shares that her Mimi, **PATRICIA ANN ALLEY** (Brentwood, Tennessee), loves to cook; but every Friday night, Mimi and Granddaddy have a "peanut butter party." The menu consists of half a peanut butter and banana sandwich, dill pickles, sliced cheese, and chocolate milk!

I pound bacon

I container (8 ounces) sour cream

I cup mayonnaise

5 cups shredded iceberg lettuce

I can (15 ounces) Le Sueur peas

$1/3$ cup sliced green onions

6 large eggs, hard-boiled and sliced

$1/2$ cup grated Parmesan cheese

1 Fry the bacon in a skillet until crisp. Drain the grease, blot on paper towels, crumble, and set aside.

2 Combine the sour cream and mayonnaise in a small bowl.

3 Place the lettuce in the bottom of a 13 x 9-inch glass baking pan. Place the peas on top of the lettuce. Next, top with the green onions. Spread the sour cream and mayonnaise mixture on top, spreading it all the way to the edges of the dish. Top with the sliced eggs, bacon, and cheese. Cover and refrigerate for 24 hours before serving.

MAKES 10 TO 12 SERVINGS.

WISE AND OTHERWISE APRICOT SALAD

Hannah Turner Lavey (Nashville, Tennessee) shares that her Grandmama, **Bernice Williams Hightower**, was a member of the Wise and Otherwise Study Club for over sixty years. Born in Luverne, Alabama, on a large working farm, Grandmama later lived in Sylacauga, Alabama, for the rest of her ninety-eight years. While she was a devout Methodist, Hannah says she loved to tell the story of tasting a Pabst Blue Ribbon beer at the 1933 World's Fair in Chicago. She would laugh and say, "Well, I don't think I'm missing anything." Another great saying of Grandmama's was, "I never get too excited or too low—no reason to get too carried away."

---

1 can (20 ounces)
  crushed pineapple

2 cans (12 ounces)
  apricots

1 envelope
  (1 tablespoon)
  unflavored gelatin

2 packages
  (3 ounces each)
  apricot gelatin

1 container
  (16 ounces) sour
  cream

---

1 Drain the pineapple and apricots, reserving the juice. Heat the juice in a small saucepan and dissolve the packages of gelatin in the juice. Allow the gelatin mixture to cool.

2 Mash the apricots or blend them lightly in a blender with a little of the sour cream. In a large bowl mix the apricots with the crushed pineapple and the remaining sour cream.

3 Add the fruit mixture to the cooled gelatin and mix well. Spoon the salad into a mold and let it congeal in the refrigerator for at least 3 hours before serving.

MAKES 10 TO 12 SERVINGS.

NANNY'S BRIDAL SALAD

JIMMIE KAY FINCH (Arlington, Tennessee) shares that this salad was one of her great-Nanny's favorites. Nanny was **CLARA LILLIAN VERNON WADE** (Fort Smith, Arkansas). Jimmie Kay says, "It seems that everyone in the family would use the same recipes, yet 'so-and-so' had the best version and you'd best be careful what you said about any dish—cooking was serious business and you might hurt someone's feelings if you picked the wrong one. We all look back on this and think it was and still is hilarious!"

2 1/2 cups hot water

1 package (3 ounces) lime gelatin

1 package (3 ounces) lemon gelatin

1/3 cup canned crushed pineapple, drained

2/3 cup evaporated milk

3/4 cup cottage cheese

1 In a large bowl mix the hot water with both packages of gelatin. Stir until the gelatin dissolves and then cool in the refrigerator approximately 20 minutes.

2 When the gelatin begins to thicken, add the pineapple, milk, and cottage cheese and mix well. Refrigerate uncovered until firm, about 60 minutes.

MAKES 6 TO 8 SERVINGS.

THREE-BEAN SALAD

MADELINE MASON (Nashville, Tennessee) says that her Gran, **EILEEN SHERRILL**, was born and raised in Port Arthur, Texas. She currently lives in Peachtree City, Georgia. Gran makes many great things to eat and her three-bean salad is a staple at every summer cookout.

I can (14.5 ounces) green beans, drained

I can (14.5 ounces) wax beans, drained

I can (16 ounces) dark red kidney beans, drained

1/2 cup chopped onion

1/2 cup chopped green bell pepper

1/2 cup vegetable oil

1/2 cup red wine vinegar (or 1/4 cup red wine vinegar plus 1/4 cup balsamic vinegar)

3/4 cup sugar

I teaspoon salt

1/4 teaspoon black pepper

---

1 In a medium bowl combine the beans, onion, and green pepper.
2 In a blender combine the oil, vinegar, sugar, salt, and pepper.
3 Pour the dressing over the vegetables and toss well. Cover and refrigerate at least 12 hours before serving.

MAKES 4 TO 6 SERVINGS.

SAWDUST SALAD

SUZANNE WORRELL (Cookeville, Tennessee) says that her Granny Bert, **BERTHA EMERSON** (Sparta, Tennessee), was a very elegant and proper lady and a dedicated homemaker, cooking three full meals a day. "She had a huge garden and grew her own vegetables," Suzanne recalls. "As a child, my favorite thing was to chop cabbage in a wooden box for sauerkraut. I learned many things from her, but the greatest lesson she taught our family was to live and survive by doing things yourself. I miss her to this day."

- 2 cans (8 ounces each) crushed pineapple with juice
- 4 heaping teaspoons all-purpose flour
- I 1/2 cups sugar
- 4 large eggs

- I package (3 ounces) lemon gelatin
- I package (3 ounces) orange gelatin
- 2 cups boiling water
- 3 medium bananas, sliced

- I package (8 ounces) cream cheese, softened
- I container (8 ounces) whipped topping, thawed
- 2 tablespoons shredded Cheddar cheese (optional)

1 Drain the crushed pineapple, reserving the juice in a saucepan. In a saucepan combine the pineapple juice, flour, sugar, and eggs. Boil until the mixture becomes a thick custard. Set it aside to cool.

2 In a separate bowl, dissolve the two packages of gelatin in the boiling water. Pour the gelatin into a 13 x 9-inch glass baking pan and let it cool.

3 When cool, add the crushed pineapple and bananas and cover. Refrigerate for 30 to 40 minutes, until congealed.

4 When congealed, spread the custard on top of the gelatin, recover, and return the dish to the refrigerator for 30 minutes.

5 In a small bowl combine the softened cream cheese and the whipped topping until well blended. Spread the mixture on top of the layered gelatin and custard, recover, and refrigerate at least 2 hours before serving. If desired, sprinkle with cheese before serving.

MAKES 6 TO 8 SERVINGS.

BETTY KEELING WOOTEN (Nashville, Tennessee) is known as B. G. to granddaughter **KATHERINE PAIGE HELTSLEY** (also of Nashville). Kate loves eating this sweet slaw with hush puppies (page 47) at B. G.'s lake house in Camden, Tennessee, and she loves to sleep in the bunk beds there while B. G. reads bedtime stories to Kate, her little brother, and her cousins.

½ cup raisins

1 medium Granny
    Smith apple,
    peeled, cored, and
    chopped

1 tablespoon sugar

½ cup mayonnaise

1 medium onion,
    finely chopped

1 head cabbage,
    shredded (3 cups)

---

1 Cover the raisins with warm water in a small bowl to plump them up. After 5 minutes, drain and place them in a large bowl.

2 Add the apple, sugar, mayonnaise, and onion to the bowl and mix well. Add the cabbage and toss. Cover and refrigerate for at least 2 hours. Serve cold.

MAKES 6 TO 8 SERVINGS.

B. B.'s Turnip Greens	K. K.'s Creamed Corn
Black-Eyed Peas	Granny's Corn Casserole
Carrot Casserole	Fried Green Tomatoes
Glazed Carrots	Southern Green Beans
Nannie's Eggplant Soufflé	Corn and Green Bean Casserole
Noonie's Zucchini Casserole	Granny Louise's Dressing
Nana's Cauliflower	Thanksgiving Cornbread-Mushroom Dressing
GG's Squash Casserole	
Squash Fritters	Oyster Loaf
Spicy Sweet Potatoes	Peas 'n' Dumplins
Make-Ahead Mashed Potatoes	Garlic Cheese Grits
"Fried" Corn	Grannie's Mac 'n' Cheese

Side Dishes

B. B.'S TURNIP GREENS

LORAN GARTNER JOHNSON (Hendersonville, Tennessee) loves her B. B.'s country cooking. B. B. is **BETTY KEELING WOOTEN** (Nashville, Tennessee). Loran, her brother, and her cousins have fond memories of sitting on B. B.'s knee and giggling as she bounced them and sang the "Poor Ol' Man" song. She would sing "Poor ol' man he rides in walk . . . poor ol' man walk . . . gentleman trot . . . ladies pace . . . soldiers gallop . . ." till the bounces got superfast!

---

4 bunches (2 ½ pounds) turnip greens	½ pound country ham, finely chopped	⅛ teaspoon crushed red pepper flakes
4 cups water, divided		

---

1 Wash the greens thoroughly in cold water. Drain the greens and cut off the tough stems and any discolored leaves.

2 In a large pot cover the greens with 2 cups water and boil for 4 to 5 minutes. Pour off the water, put the greens in 2 cups fresh water, and bring to a boil.

3 Add the ham and red pepper flakes. Reduce the heat, cover, and simmer for 40 minutes, or until the greens are tender—they should look like cooked spinach. Serve with pepper vinegar and hard-boiled eggs, if desired.

MAKES 6 SERVINGS.

BLACK-EYED PEAS

KIM HOFFMAN (Hendersonville, Tennessee) says that Grandma, **BUNA JORDAN**, was a true Southern lady, born and raised in southern Alabama. "I used to love sitting on the porch with her shelling field peas." Kim recalls. "Grandma could make a full-course meal in twenty minutes using nothing but what was already available in her kitchen. It did not impress me then; but I'm so impressed now, especially when it takes me half a day and I've got a grocery list a mile long!"

2 tablespoons olive oil

4 cloves garlic, minced

I medium onion, finely diced

I bay leaf

I pound fresh or frozen black-eyed peas

6 cups vegetable broth

1/4 teaspoon salt

1/4 teaspoon black pepper

2 teaspoons chopped fresh parsley

1 Pour the oil into a large skillet over medium-high heat. Add the garlic, onion, and bay leaf and sauté until tender and fragrant.

2 Add the black-eyed peas and broth. Simmer until the peas are tender, 25 to 30 minutes. Season with the salt and pepper. Serve the peas warm and garnish with the parsley.

MAKES 6 SERVINGS.

CARROT CASSEROLE

ABIGAIL KAREN DOUCET (Ruther Glen, Virginia) will never personally know her maternal grandma, **KAREN SUE GREGG WILLHOIT** (Falmouth, Virginia), who unfortunately lost her battle to breast cancer in 2001. However, mom **LEIGH WILLHOIT DOUCET** will do her best to make sure Abigail and her stepsisters know all about Karen and how she lived her life. "Family time was really important to Karen and she tried to cook mostly healthy things," Leigh says. "She made a lot of casseroles and dishes with fresh veggies. Weekend mornings were always big breakfast days for us too."

2 pounds carrots

1/2 stick butter

2 cups shredded
    Cheddar cheese

1/4 cup milk

2 eggs, beaten

I teaspoon onion salt

I teaspoon sugar

cooking spray

1 Preheat the oven to 350 degrees.

2 Boil the carrots in water in a large saucepan for approximately 25 minutes. Drain the carrots and mash in a large bowl. Add the butter and cheese and mix until melted. Add the milk, eggs, onion salt, and sugar and mix well.

3 Lightly spray a 2-quart casserole dish with cooking spray. Spoon the carrot mixture into the casserole dish.

4 Bake uncovered for 30 minutes or until heated through. Serve warm.

MAKES 6 SERVINGS.

GLAZED CARROTS

"My two sisters and I live not far from where our Grammy lived," says **EMMA GREGG** (Richmond, Kentucky). Grammy was **ESTHER ELAINE FERKAN GREGG** (Lexington, Kentucky) and she passed away in 2008. Emma says, "She used to sew things for us and always had good food and snacks for us to eat. We miss her a lot."

I stick butter

3 pounds baby carrots (about 120 carrots)

1/3 cup vinegar

2 tablespoons brown sugar

4 tablespoons white sugar

1/8 teaspoon salt

1/4 teaspoon black pepper

1/3 cup chopped fresh chives

1 Melt the butter in a Dutch oven or large nonstick pot over medium-high heat. Sauté the carrots until slightly tender, about 10 minutes.

2 Stir in the vinegar, brown sugar, and white sugar and mix to coat. Cook for 7 to 10 minutes, until the carrots are glazed and tender. Season with the salt and pepper. Add the chives and toss before serving.

MAKES 8 SERVINGS.

NANNIE'S EGGPLANT SOUFFLÉ

"A whistlin' woman and a crowing hen, both will come to no good end," is something her Nannie used to say, recalls **PRISCILLA TUCKER** (Dothan, Alabama). Nannie, **RUBY KATE McKOON ANTHONY LAWSON**, was born in Woodbury, Georgia, and lived most of her life in Vero Beach, Florida. Nannie ran a boarding house and, although she did not provide meals to her boarders, if anyone did not have a place to go for the holidays she made sure they were at her table. Holidays had to have at least three meats—turkey, ham, and often duck. Nannie loved to bake bread and, for year, she even churned her own butter.

I medium eggplant, peeled and diced

I cup plus 3 tablespoons bread crumbs, divided

1/2 stick butter, divided

2 large eggs, separated

1/2 cup shredded mozzarella cheese

1/4 cup diced onion

1/4 teaspoon salt

1/4 teaspoon black pepper

1 Preheat the oven to 350 degrees.
2 In a saucepan cook the eggplant in salted water until tender. Drain the eggplant.
3 In a large bowl combine the eggplant, I cup of the bread crumbs, 3 tablespoons of the butter, the egg yolks, cheese, onion, salt, and pepper. In a small bowl beat the egg whites until stiff. Fold the egg whites into the eggplant and bread crumb mixture. Spoon the eggplant mixture into a 9-inch baking dish.
4 Melt the remaining I tablespoon butter and mix it with the remaining 3 tablespoons of bread crumbs in a small bowl. Top the eggplant with the buttered bread crumbs.
5 Bake for 30 minutes until bubbly and the top is lightly browned.

MAKES 4 TO 6 SERVINGS.

NOONIE'S ZUCCHINI CASSEROLE

"Sometimes the simplest ingredients can create the best dishes. Always made with fresh zucchini from her garden, this recipe was a summer staple for my Noonie, **LINDA PARKER** (Morehead, Kentucky). I used to help her get fresh veggies from the garden—it always seemed like there was way too much zucchini. While I liked to help pick the things we were going to cook with, I wasn't big on the weeding part," shares **SUSAN MILLER** (Nashville, Tennessee).

---

2 tablespoons butter

4 medium zucchini, sliced 1/4-inch thick

I large onion, thinly sliced

I teaspoon onion salt

1/4 teaspoon dried oregano

I can (8 ounces) tomato sauce

I cup shredded mozzarella cheese

---

1 Preheat the oven to 350 degrees.

2 Melt the butter and sauté the zucchini and onion until tender. Add the onion salt, oregano, and tomato sauce.

3 Pour the mixture into a I 1/2-quart shallow casserole dish. Top with the cheese.

4 Bake for 30 minutes.

MAKES 6 SERVINGS.

NANA'S CAULIFLOWER

A true Southern lady all her life, Nana, **ANITA SHERRILL**, was born and raised in Hattiesburg, Mississippi, and currently lives in Peachtree City, Georgia. Granddaughter **ALYSSA MADDOX** (Nashville, Tennessee) shares that Nana loves this cauliflower recipe because, as Nana says, "Almost every recipe is better with cheese on it!"

1 medium head cauliflower

1/3 cup water

3/4 cup mayonnaise

1/2 cup finely chopped onion

1/2 teaspoon prepared mustard

1/4 teaspoon salt

3/4 cup shredded Cheddar cheese

1 Remove the leaves and the stem from the cauliflower and lightly trim the core. Wash the cauliflower well and cut into florets.

2 Place the cauliflower in a microwave-safe dish (with a lid). Add the water, cover, and cook on high in the microwave for about 9 minutes. Test the cauliflower with a fork to see if it is tender. When it is done, drain off the water.

3 In a separate small bowl, mix the mayonnaise, onion, mustard, and salt to form a paste. Spread the mixture over the cauliflower. Top with the cheese. Microwave uncovered on high for 2 to 3 minutes, or until the cheese is melted.

MAKES 3 TO 4 SERVINGS.

GG'S SQUASH CASSEROLE

ALAINA PLAUCHÉ (Wilmington, North Carolina) calls her grandmother GG. GG is **DIANE PLAUCHÉ** (Columbus, Georgia). "We can count on GG making this incredible squash casserole every year for Thanksgiving dinner," Alaina says. "My mama, Laura, says that she came up with this recipe; but really, GG started it. She lets my mom think that because she's a nice GG."

---

1 pound yellow summer squash

1 pound zucchini

2 large eggs, beaten

½ cup evaporated milk

3 tablespoons sugar

1 teaspoon salt

1 stick plus 1 tablespoon butter, divided

1 large onion, chopped

2 cups shredded Cheddar or Colby Jack cheese

1 cup crushed Ritz crackers

---

1 Preheat the oven to 350 degrees.

2 In a medium saucepan cook the yellow squash and zucchini in salted water until tender. Drain well and mash in a large bowl.

3 Add the eggs, milk, sugar, salt, 6 tablespoons of the butter, onion, and cheese to the squash. Mix well and pour into a 2-quart casserole dish.

4 Bake uncovered for 25 minutes.

5 **TO MAKE THE TOPPING**, melt the remaining 3 tablespoons of butter and combine with the crushed crackers in a small bowl. Sprinkle the crushed cracker mixture on top of the casserole and continue baking for another 10 to 15 minutes, or until browned on top.

MAKES 4 TO 6 SERVINGS.

SQUASH FRITTERS

LAURA TROUP (Nashville, Tennessee) shares that her grandmother's squash fritters recipe is one that has been passed down for generations. Her mother taught her the proper grating technique, how to mix all the ingredients to get the right texture, how to gently drop the spoonfuls into the fatback grease, and exactly what color the fritters needed to be before turning them over. This recipe became famous—her grandmother, **ELIZABETH POSEY** (Florence, Alabama), even agreed for it to be used in a fund-raising cookbook for a local school. Laura says, "Grandmother taught me as a child how to follow a recipe by using that cookbook open next to the stove, and the page with that recipe has the grease-spatter evidence of our meticulous lessons. She left me the cookbook when she died. Even though everyone in my family knows this recipe by heart, I always use the cookbook when I make squash fritters at home because those pages hold a special place in my heart for her."

2 cups grated yellow summer squash	1 medium onion, grated	salt and black pepper to taste
2 tablespoons butter, melted	6 tablespoons all-purpose flour	vegetable oil for frying
2 large eggs, beaten	2 teaspoons sugar	

1 In a large bowl mix the squash, butter, eggs, onion, flour, sugar, salt, and pepper.

2 Heat the oil in a large skillet and drop the mixture by tablespoonfuls into the hot oil. Cook in batches, if necessary. Cook until brown, turn, and cook the other side until brown. Drain on paper towels.

MAKES 4 SERVINGS.

SPICY SWEET POTATOES

"Spending time at Nanny's was the absolute best," says **LYNN WHITE** (Tulsa, Oklahoma). "She loved her sweets and as I look through so many of her recipes, I find a sugary element to many of them." Lynn recalls that Nanny, **DORIS MATTHEWS** (Birmingham, Alabama), always had an "ask and you shall receive" attitude in her kitchen and home. Lynn says, "She was most content when making somebody happy with something she created in her kitchen. If she gave us cookies or a slice of her homemade cake or pie, she'd often say 'something sweet for my sweets,' the sweets being us kids, of course."

---

6 pounds sweet potatoes (about 12 medium), unpeeled

1/3 cup maple syrup

3/4 cup sour cream

4 teaspoons chipotle chilies, pureed

1 1/2 teaspoons ground cinnamon

1/4 teaspoon salt

---

1 Boil the sweet potatoes in a large pot of water until soft (or bake at 375 degrees for 50 to 60 minutes).
2 In the meantime, combine the maple syrup, sour cream, chipotle puree, cinnamon, and salt in a small bowl. Whisk until smooth.
3 When the potatoes are cooked and soft, remove the peel and mash with a potato masher. Add the maple syrup and sour cream mixture to the potatoes and blend well. Serve warm.

MAKES 12 SERVINGS.

MAKE-AHEAD MASHED POTATOES

HANNAH CATHERINE CAUDILL (Franklin, Tennessee) calls her grandma SaSa. **SARA CAUDILL** was born in Greenville, Alabama, and now lives in Dickson, Tennessee. When a serving dish at the table starts to get empty, her children and grandchildren will say, "The dish is leaking."

4 pounds potatoes, unpeeled

1/2 stick (1/4 cup) butter

1 package (8 ounces) cream cheese, softened

1 container (8 ounces) sour cream

1/3 cup milk

1 1/2 teaspoons salt

1 teaspoon black pepper

2 tablespoons butter, melted

2 tablespoons minced fresh chives (optional)

1 Put the potatoes in a large pot and add water to cover, plus an additional inch. Cover and bring to a boil. Reduce the heat and simmer for 25 minutes or until tender. Drain and peel the potatoes.

2 Place the potatoes in a large bowl and mash with a potato masher. Stir in 1/4 cup butter, the cream cheese, sour cream, milk, salt, and pepper.

3 Spoon the potatoes into a greased 13 x 9-inch baking pan. Brush the top of the potatoes with the melted butter. Cover and refrigerate for at least 12 hours.

4 Remove from the refrigerator and let stand at room temperature for 30 minutes.

5 Preheat the oven to 350 degrees. Bake for 40 minutes, or until thoroughly heated. Garnish with the chives, if desired.

MAKES 12 SERVINGS.

"FRIED" CORN

GALE TAYLOR (Starkville, Mississippi) called her grandma Mamaw Cummings. Mamaw Cummings, **BELL GOOCH CUMMINGS** (Friendship, Pontotoc County, Mississippi), would say, "Let me kiss your hand," whenever Gale would either enter or leave her house. Gale says, "I always look back and remember that it seemed funny to me that she always called her husband 'Mr. William.' I never heard her call him anything different and it was enriched with respect and admiration. Although the corn in this recipe is not really fried, Mamaw called it that, probably to fool us into trying it the first time. We didn't need to be coaxed after one bite! She lived right next door to us, which meant that I was there all the time. I can remember shucking and silking fresh corn on the back porch and always hoped this recipe would be the outcome of that work."

- 8 ears fresh corn, shucked and silked
- 1 1/2 cups water
- 3 tablespoons all-purpose flour
- 2 teaspoons sugar
- 1 teaspoon salt
- 1/4 teaspoon black pepper
- 3 tablespoons bacon drippings

1. Over a large bowl cut the corn from the cob using a sharp knife. Discard the cobs. Stir in the water, flour, sugar, salt, and pepper and mix well.
2. In a large cast-iron skillet, melt the bacon drippings over medium-low heat. When hot, add the corn mixture and reduce the heat to low. Cook uncovered, stirring occasionally, for 40 minutes. Serve hot.

MAKES 6 SERVINGS.

K. K.'S CREAMED CORN

MANDY HELTSLEY BUTTERS (Nashville, Tennessee) says that her grandmother, K. K., **KATHERINE KEELING** (formerly of Tullahoma, Tennessee, and now of Nashville), made her creamed corn with Hickory Cane corn—which is virtually impossible to find now. (At one time Hickory Cane corn was grown, mainly in the Appalachian Mountains, to be made into white cornmeal, hominy, and moonshine, since it had a higher sugar content than field corn. It has a warm, nutty flavor and very large kernels.) K. K. says to be sure and add salt and lots of butter and pepper when you make this creamed corn. Mandy recalls being about seven when she and K. K. bought fifteen ears from a farmer—and fifteen ears are a lot for one lady to shuck and tip. Mandy remembers a big mess with corn milk and pulp everywhere. She says, "K. K. almost couldn't finish and asked all of us to help because she needed more muscles to get the scraping part done right."

---

6 medium ears fresh corn, shucked and silked

1/2 stick butter, divided

1/4 cup water

1/2 teaspoon salt

1/2 teaspoon black pepper

1/2 cup milk or cream

I tablespoon all-purpose flour (optional)

Crumbled bacon (optional)

---

1 "Tip" the corn into a large skillet. Tip it by cutting the kernels halfway off (meaning that the bottom half of each kernel is left on the cob and the top half is cut off). Using the back of the knife, scrape the cob so the milk comes out and the pulp comes off.

2 Melt 2 tablespoons of the butter in the skillet with the corn and corn milk. Add the water and cook until done, stirring constantly, 10 to 12 minutes. Stir in the salt, pepper, and the remaining 2 tablespoons of butter. Gradually add the milk, stirring constantly. The starch in the corn should naturally thicken it. If you need to make it thicker, add I tablespoon of flour. Cook a few minutes longer and be careful not to boil. Serve hot and garnish with crumbled bacon, if desired.

MAKES 6 SERVINGS.

GRANNY'S CORN CASSEROLE

JENNIFER MITCHELL (Murfreesboro, Tennessee) shares that her Granny, **CLAUDIA MITCHELL**, was born in Spencer, Tennessee, and now lives in McMinnville, Tennessee. Jennifer says, "Granny always made this corn casserole for every family gathering and it always conjures up good memories when I eat it or think about it." Jennifer also shares that her Granny and Papa's Saturday evening ritual was to eat cornbread dipped in buttermilk while watching wrestling.

5 large eggs

1/3 cup butter, melted

1/4 cup sugar

1/2 cup milk

1/4 cup cornstarch

1 can (15.25 ounces) whole-kernel corn

2 cans (14.75 ounces each) creamed corn

1 Preheat the oven to 400 degrees.

2 In a large bowl lightly beat the eggs. Add the melted butter, sugar, and milk. Whisk in the cornstarch. Stir in the corn and creamed corn. Blend well. Pour the mixture into a greased 2-quart casserole dish.

3 Bake for 60 minutes, or until done when a knife inserted in the center comes out moist, but not wet.

MAKES 6 TO 8 SERVINGS.

SARAH SMITH (Tupelo, Mississippi) was named for her grandmother, **SARAH LANGSTON** (Saltillo, Mississippi). She and her siblings called their grandmother Mammy. Mammy had a small garden where she grew most of the vegetables for her family to eat. Sarah shares that tomatoes were grown and sold as a source of income. "When we were little we would pick a few green tomatoes that 'forced' grandmother to fry us up some fried green tomatoes," Sarah says. "Like most women trying to feed a farming family, she always cooked meals in large quantities. There were always three hot meals a day served around the Langston house."

---

2 large eggs, beaten

1/2 cup milk

1/2 cup cornmeal

1/2 cup all-purpose flour

4 green tomatoes, sliced 1/4-inch thick

vegetable oil for frying

1/4 teaspoon salt

---

1 Beat the eggs and milk in a small bowl. Combine the cornmeal and flour in a separate small bowl. Dredge the tomato slices through the milk and egg mixture and then coat each side with the cornmeal and flour mixture.

2 Heat the oil in a large skillet and fry the tomatoes, turning gently, until golden brown, about 3 minutes per side. Drain on paper towels to absorb the excess oil. Lightly salt before serving. Serve hot.

MAKES 6 TO 8 SERVINGS.

SOUTHERN GREEN BEANS

"We always had great traditional Southern food at my grandmother's house—lots of cornbread, green beans and 'ice milk,'" shares **LAURA ELLIS** (Nashville, Tennessee). Grandmother Price, **ELEANOR CHANDLER PRICE** (Prentiss, Mississippi), was a great cook. Grandmother's cornbread often made its way into a glass of buttermilk that Laura's grandfather would eat at night. He was a farmer (as well as a teacher and a state senator). Her grandparents had a large garden, and Laura says, "There were more fresh vegetables when we were there than we were used to at home, especially green beans and tomatoes. They had a pecan tree and my siblings and I loved collecting the pecans, though shelling them took hours and our hands were always sore afterwards—we also got yelled at for eating them as fast as we could shell them."

---

3 cups fresh or frozen green beans

4 slices bacon

1/2 small onion, diced

2 cups chicken broth

1/8 teaspoon salt

1/8 teaspoon black pepper

---

1 If using fresh green beans, remove the ends, snap the beans in half, and rinse.

2 In a large saucepan cook the bacon over medium-high heat until it begins to brown. Add the onion and cook until softened, stirring occasionally. When the bacon is done, remove, drain on paper towels, and crumble.

3 Add the bacon back to the saucepan. Add the fresh or frozen green beans and sauté with the cooked bacon and onion. Add the broth, salt, and pepper. Bring to a boil, reduce the heat, cover, and simmer for 20 minutes, or until the beans are very tender.

MAKES 4 SERVINGS.

CORN AND GREEN BEAN CASSEROLE

MADISON FLOURNOY (Franklin, Tennessee) shares that her Nana's corn and green bean casserole is a family favorite that has a presence during each Thanksgiving and Christmas meal. While she lost her Nana, **MAUDE ROBINS COBB FLOURNOY** (Hampton, Virginia), many years ago, Madison says, "I have a relationship with her through what I hear, and of course, what I eat. When I'm cooking, I like to think she is right there cooking with me."

1 can (11 ounces) shoepeg corn, drained

1 can (14.5 ounces) green beans, drained

1/2 cup chopped celery

1/2 cup chopped onion

1 cup shredded Cheddar cheese

1/2 cup sour cream

1 can (10.75 ounces) cream of celery soup

1 can (5 ounces) sliced water chestnuts

2 sleeves Ritz crackers, crushed

1/2 stick butter, melted

1/2 cup slivered almonds

1 Preheat the oven to 350 degrees.

2 In a large bowl mix the corn, beans, celery, onion, cheese, sour cream, soup, and water chestnuts. Spoon the mixture into a lightly greased 2-quart casserole dish.

3 In a medium bowl mix the crushed crackers, melted butter, and almonds. Sprinkle the cracker mixture on top of the casserole.

4 Bake for 30 to 45 minutes, or until the topping is lightly browned and the casserole is heated throughout.

MAKES 6 TO 8 SERVINGS.

GRANNY LOUISE'S DRESSING

Jo McCloud (Chattanooga, Tennessee) recalls that her Granny, **Louise Hollis** (also of Chattanooga), had some great sayings. Two of her favorites were "One hundred years from now nobody will remember" and "You're enough to make a preacher cuss." Jo says that Granny taught her to cook and she kept the whole family entertained.

5 cups crumbled
cornbread

3 cups crumbled
toasted bread

1 1/2 sticks butter,
melted

1 cup chopped onions

3/4 cup chopped
celery

2 large eggs, beaten

1/4 teaspoon black
pepper

1/2 teaspoon dried
thyme

1 1/4 teaspoons dried
sage

3/4 teaspoon salt

2 cups chicken or
turkey broth

1 Preheat the oven to 350 degrees.

2 Place the cornbread and crumbled toasted bread in a large bowl.

3 In a medium skillet heat the butter and sauté the onions and celery for about 10 minutes, or until tender. Pour the butter and vegetable mixture over the cornbread and bread mixture.

4 In a small bowl combine the eggs, pepper, thyme, sage, and salt and mix well. Pour the egg mixture over the cornbread and bread combination and mix well. Add enough broth to make the whole mixture very moist. Spoon the dressing into a greased 13 x 9-inch baking pan.

5 Bake uncovered for 60 minutes, or until set firm.

MAKES 8 TO 10 SERVINGS.

THANKSGIVING CORNBREAD-MUSHROOM DRESSING

Gran, **EILEEN SHERRILL**, was born and raised in Port Arthur, Texas. She currently lives in Peachtree City, Georgia, but visits Nashville often to see granddaughter **MADELINE MASON**. Gran has made Madeline many homemade quilts, which are priceless treasures. This recipe was handed down from Gran's mother, but over the years Gran has adapted it and made it her own. This dressing is, of course, an important part of each Thanksgiving dinner.

5 slices bacon, cooked and crumbled

1 tablespoon olive oil

1 stick butter

4 celery stalks, chopped

1 cup chopped green bell pepper

1 large white or yellow onion, chopped

4 cloves garlic, chopped

8 ounces fresh mushrooms, sliced

1 pan (8 x 8 inches) cornbread, crumbled

1 package (14 ounces) herb stuffing mix

1 cup cooked rice

1 tablespoon chopped fresh rosemary, sage, parsley, and thyme

1 cup chopped green onions

6 large eggs, hard-boiled and chopped

1 turkey giblet, chopped

5 cups turkey or chicken broth

1 Preheat the oven to 375 degrees.

2 In a large skillet fry the bacon, rendering much of the fat. Remove the bacon and cool.

3 Add the oil and butter to the bacon fat in the skillet. Add the celery, green pepper, and onion and sauté until tender. Add the garlic and mushrooms and sauté for about 1 1/2 minutes.

4 In a large bowl mix the cornbread, stuffing mix or bread crumbs, and rice. Next, add the sautéed vegetables and crumbled bacon. Add the rosemary, sage, parsley, thyme, green onions, hard-boiled eggs, and giblet meat and mix well. Pack the mixture into a 13 x 9-inch baking dish and moisten well with the broth.

5 Bake uncovered for 30 to 40 minutes until lightly brown on top.

MAKES 10 TO 12 SERVINGS.

OYSTER LOAF ❈ ❈

Grandmother Price, **ELEANOR CHANDLER PRICE** (Prentiss, Mississippi), was a great cook, shares granddaughter **LAURA ELLIS** (Nashville, Tennessee). Laura says, "This oyster loaf is the one recipe that truly says 'Prentiss, Mississippi' to me, and for my mom's family, the oyster loaf is a staple at Thanksgiving and Christmas meals. And no worries, it tastes much better than the title sounds!"

---

1 pint fresh shucked oysters, with liquid, finely chopped

2 large eggs, well beaten

1 1/2 cups plus 3 tablespoons saltine cracker crumbs, divided

5 tablespoons butter, divided

1 1/2 cups chopped celery

1 cup chopped fresh parsley

1 small onion, chopped

1/8 teaspoon salt

1/4 teaspoon black pepper

---

1 Preheat the oven to 350 degrees.

2 In a large bowl mix the oysters and liquid, eggs, and 1 1/2 cups of the cracker crumbs.

3 In a large skillet melt 3 tablespoons of the butter and wilt the celery, parsley, and onion.

4 Add the vegetable mixture to the oyster mixture and mix well. Add the salt and pepper and mix well. Spoon into a lightly greased 1 1/2-quart baking dish. Cover with the remaining 3 tablespoons cracker crumbs. Dot well with the remaining 2 tablespoons butter.

5 Bake uncovered for 15 minutes, or until browned on top. Serve as you would a side dish or dressing/stuffing.

MAKES 4 TO 5 SERVINGS.

ALLYSON ADAMS JOHNSON (Hendersonville, Tennessee) remembers that when her grandmother K. K., **KATHERINE KEELING**, lived in Tullahoma, Tennessee, she had this beat-up, heavy, old dough table with a lid and a marble top in her kitchen. When she wasn't making dumplings, it served as counter space. Allyson says that when K. K. was making dumplings, the kids loved to watch. K. K. would roll the dumplings out on the dough table and then close the lid so they could dry out overnight. K. K. now lives in Nashville and Allyson's little girl, Lauren, also loves great-grandma K. K.'s peas and dumplings.

DUMPLINGS:

1 ½ cups all-purpose flour

1 large egg, beaten

¼ teaspoon salt

¼ cup milk

BROTH:

1 quart water

3 slices bacon

1 pound fresh or frozen peas

½ stick butter

¼ teaspoon black pepper

½ teaspoon dried parsley

1 **TO MAKE THE DUMPLINGS,** put the flour in a large bowl, making a well in the middle. Add the egg and salt and mix well. Add the milk and combine, making a sticky dough with the consistency of bread dough. Spread a thick layer of flour on a work surface and roll out the dumplings as thin as you can get them. Loosely cover with clean cotton dish towels and allow to dry out overnight.

2 **TO MAKE THE BROTH,** boil the water with the bacon in a large pot. Cook until the grease floats to the top. Leave the grease in. Add the peas, butter, black pepper, and parsley to the boiling water.

3 Cut the dumplings into 2-inch-wide strips. Pinch off 2 inches at a time from each strip and add to the boiling pea mixture. The dumplings will absorb the grease and butter. Reduce the heat to medium and cook for 20 minutes. After 20 minutes, taste the peas and dumplings for desired tenderness.

MAKES 4 TO 5 SERVINGS.

GARLIC CHEESE GRITS

Nana, **VENICE WILSON**, was a true Southern lady, born and raised in Mayfield, Kentucky, shares **MARY ANN LAWSON** (Nashville, Tennessee). "Nana was a great cook and I learned so much from both her and my mom about preparing food," Mary Ann says. "I used to pull my chair up to the kitchen counter and stand next to her so I could watch her cook and bake."

---

4 ½ cups boiling water

I cup quick-cooking grits

I teaspoon salt

I clove garlic, minced

I stick butter

3 cups shredded Cheddar cheese

2 eggs

3/4 cup milk (approximately)

---

1 Preheat the oven to 350 degrees.
2 Combine the water, grits, salt, and garlic in a large saucepan. Cook until the grits are slightly thick, 10 minutes or more.
3 In a medium saucepan cook the butter and cheese on low heat until melted.
4 Break the eggs into a glass measuring cup. Pour in enough milk on top of the eggs to measure I cup and mix well. Pour the egg and milk mixture into the medium saucepan with the cheese mixture and mix well.
5 Pour the egg, milk, and cheese mixture into the hot grits and mix well. Pour the grits into a 9 x 8-inch baking pan.
6 Bake uncovered for 45 minutes or until bubbling.

MAKES 4 SERVINGS.

GRANNIE'S MAC 'N' CHEESE

"This is not your typical macaroni and cheese!" says **LISA GLASER** (Nashville, Tennessee). This baked macaroni casserole uses sharp Cheddar cheese, eggs, and milk for a great crusty top. The onion, mustard, and paprika give it just a little "bite" and are precisely what helped to make it a favorite side dish at Grannie's table. Grannie, **NELLIE MAE SWINT** (Augusta, Georgia), was a part of the Richmond County Sheriff's Department. As a deputy, she was assigned the job of school crossing guard, which was one of the few departmental jobs available to women at that time. Lisa says, "Working at one of the busiest intersections in Augusta, Grannie was known and loved by the many school children that she 'put across the road.' After Grannie retired, I'd rummage through an old Whitman Sampler box where she kept school portraits, many of which were old and turning brown with age. Even though most of the pictures bore no names, Grannie remembered them all. I'd hold up a photo and she'd say, 'Oh, that's little Bobby so-and-so—he's the president of the bank now.' Grannie kept that box of photos until she passed away."

---

2 cups elbow macaroni, uncooked

1/2 stick butter

2 1/2 cups shredded sharp Cheddar cheese, divided

2 large eggs

1/2 cup milk

1/2 teaspoon dry mustard

1/4 cup minced onion

1 tablespoon paprika

---

1 Preheat the oven to 350 degrees.
2 Cook the macaroni according to the package directions. Drain the macaroni well and then return it to the pot you cooked it in. Add the butter and stir until completely melted. Add 2 cups of the cheese.
3 In a separate bowl whisk the eggs with the milk. Stir in the mustard and onion.
4 Pour the egg mixture over the macaroni and stir well. Pour the macaroni into a lightly greased 8-inch square baking pan. Top with the remaining 1/2 cup of cheese and sprinkle the paprika on top.
5 Bake uncovered for 30 minutes, or until the cheese has melted and browned.

MAKES 4 TO 6 SERVINGS.

Miss Clara's Shrimp Gumbo (page 164)

Main Dishes

Busy-Day Pork
Casserole

Ham à la Mamie

Ham and Scalloped
Potatoes

Georgia Hash

Beef Stroganoff

Company Casserole

Dixie Meat Loaf

Old-fashioned Pot Roast

Steak and Pan Gravy

Creamed Chicken on
Cornbread

Corene's Herb
Dumplings and Chicken

Botts's Brunswick Stew

Granny D's Chicken
Casserole

Chicken Puffs

Mama Grace's Chicken
'n' Dumplins

Broccoli-Chicken
Casserole

Grandmother's Deep-
Fat-Fried Chicken

Tangy Barbecued
Chicken

Chicken Potpie

Chicken-Fried Steak

Crab Cakes

Salmon Croquettes

Welsh Rarebit

Miss Clara's Shrimp
Gumbo

BUSY-DAY PORK CASSEROLE

LAURA TROUP (Nashville, Tennessee) shares that mealtime was important at the home of her grandmother, **ELIZABETH POSEY** (Florence, Alabama). "My dad attended elementary school across the street from his house and went home for a big lunch every day," Laura says. "Evening family mealtime was important in their house as well. When Granddaddy closed his store each day, he came home to a huge supper eaten around the table. Although each meal was prepared with care, Sunday lunch was the biggest meal of the week. So much time and effort went into cooking it that Grandmother often spent her entire Saturday preparing for the meal. Having the preacher over after services was a special treat."

6 pork steaks

1 1/2 tablespoons shortening

2 medium onions, sliced

1 package (16 ounces) frozen lima beans

1/2 cup milk

1/4 teaspoon poultry seasoning

1/4 teaspoon dried oregano

1/2 teaspoon salt

1/8 teaspoon black pepper

1/8 teaspoon dried thyme

1 can (10.75 ounces) cream of celery soup

1 Preheat the oven to 350 degrees.

2 In a large skillet over medium heat, brown the steaks in the shortening. Remove the steaks, keeping the drippings in the pan. Arrange the steaks in a 13 x 9-inch casserole dish.

3 Sauté the onions and beans in the pork drippings until tender. Pour off any excess drippings and spoon the onions and beans on top of the steaks.

4 In the same skillet combine the milk, poultry seasoning, oregano, salt, pepper, and thyme. Stir in the soup and mix well. Heat on medium until mixture is combined well and soup has no lumps. Pour the soup mixture over the pork, onions, and lima beans.

5 Cover and bake for 15 to 20 minutes, or until heated through. Serve warm.

MAKES 6 SERVINGS.

HAM À LA MAMIE

JESSICA SCHIMBORSKI (Mount Juliet, Tennessee) shares that this ham recipe from her Grandma Mamie, MAMIE OSBORNE (Blytheville, Arkansas), is soooo excellent. "This is the way Mamie always made ham to slice for sandwiches," Jessica says. "I have made it like this numerous times, and you can't believe how good the house smells as this simmers." Jessica also shares that Mamie was certainly a character. She'd sometimes say, "Jessica, could you make me a Pepsi 'bout as long as my arm?"

5 pounds old-fashioned smoked boneless ham

4 cloves garlic

1/2 teaspoon celery seed

1/2 teaspoon pickling spice

1 bottle (3.5 ounces) liquid smoke

1 Preheat the oven to 325 degrees.

2 Cover the ham with water in a large roasting pan. Add the garlic cloves, celery seed, pickling spice, and liquid smoke.

3 Bake for 4 hours, 2 hours on each side. Baste the ham with the pan juices every 20 to 30 minutes during baking. If using a flat-bottomed pan, put a knife under the ham to keep it from sticking. Serve warm or cold.

MAKES 6 TO 8 SERVINGS.

HAM AND SCALLOPED POTATOES

Gwen Dedrick McCoy (Hermitage, Tennessee) says that her Granny, Alice May Downey (Mobile, Alabama), loved good comfort food. Gwen recalls, "You knew you had her stamp of approval when she said, 'Well, I swanee, this is good!' As grandkids we never figured out exactly what that meant, but by the look on her face, we knew it was a good thing!"

---

1 can (10.75 ounces) cream of mushroom soup

1/4 cup milk

1/2 cup cottage cheese

1/2 cup chopped onion

1 cup shredded Swiss cheese, divided

1/2 teaspoon black pepper

1/4 teaspoon salt

5 cups potatoes, thinly sliced, divided

3 cups cubed cooked ham

2 tablespoons butter

---

1 Preheat the oven to 350 degrees.

2 In a medium bowl combine the soup, milk, cottage cheese, onion, 1/2 cup of the Swiss cheese, black pepper, and salt.

3 Place half of the potatoes in a greased shallow 2-quart casserole dish. Cover with the ham. Top with the remaining potatoes. Pour the soup mixture over the potatoes. Dot with the butter.

4 Cover and bake for about 60 minutes. Uncover and bake for 30 to 40 minutes longer, or until the potatoes are cooked through. During the last 15 minutes of baking, sprinkle the remaining 1/2 cup cheese on top of the scalloped potatoes.

MAKES 5 TO 6 SERVINGS.

Grannie served hash over slices of white bread, but it's also great over white rice or with a big hunk of cornbread, says **LISA GLASER** (Nashville, Tennessee). Even after working all day as a deputy for the Richmond County Sheriff's Department, Grannie, **NELLIE MAE SWINT** (Augusta, Georgia), would come home and cook up a big dinner for herself, her husband, and whoever else dropped by. Her home never had air-conditioning and the heat in her little kitchen could be stifling, but she'd just plug in her ancient (and loud) circulating fan, turn up the police scanner that sat on top of her refrigerator, and keep on cooking.

3 pounds beef sirloin steak, cubed

1 pound boneless, skinless chicken breasts, cubed

salt for cooking water

1 large Vidalia onion, chopped

1 large baking potato, peeled and boiled until almost done, chopped

1 can (28 ounces) whole tomatoes

1 can (15.25 ounces) white corn

1 can (15.25 ounces) yellow corn

1 cup cider vinegar

1 tablespoon crushed red pepper flakes

1 tablespoon black pepper

1 Place the beef and chicken in a large pot and add water to cover. Salt the water slightly. Simmer until the meat is tender, about 60 minutes. Remove the meat from the pot, retain the broth, and cool.

2 Using a hand grinder, coarsely grind the meat. (The meat can be chopped with a knife if no grinder is available, but don't use a food processor, as it will break down the meat too much.)

3 Place the meat back in the pot of broth. Add the onion, potato, canned tomatoes, corn, vinegar, red pepper flakes, and black pepper. Cook the mixture on medium heat until completely heated through. Continue cooking until the consistency is that of a thick stew. Serve over white bread, rice, or cornbread, if desired.

MAKES 10 SERVINGS.

❖❖❖ BEEF STROGANOFF

MADISON FLOURNOY (Franklin, Tennessee) shares that one of her most vivid memories of her childhood with her grandma, **MARGE CAMERON** (Portsmouth, Virginia), was in her mother's childhood home, where she spent many summers as a young girl. Madison says, "After the long days of make-believe and sweaty fun, I'd come into the house to the smell of my grandma's beef stroganoff. My grandmother is a full-blooded Hungarian and this is one of her traditional dishes from her heritage. I recently had the pleasure of learning how to prepare this dish with my mother and grandma by my side. It's one of the many things that keeps me connected to my Hungarian culture."

½ cup all-purpose flour

⅛ teaspoon salt

⅛ teaspoon black pepper

2 pounds beef top sirloin steak, cut into bite-size pieces

¾ cup vegetable oil, divided

2 large onions, sliced into thin rings

1 cup sliced fresh mushrooms

1 can (6 ounces) tomato paste

2 tablespoons paprika

1 container (16 ounces) sour cream

2 packages (12 ounces each) wide egg noodles

⅛ teaspoon dried parsley

---

1 Fill a large Ziploc bag with the flour, salt, and pepper. Put 6 sirloin pieces into the bag and shake until the meat is coated. Repeat until all the meat is coated.

2 In a large skillet on medium heat, heat half of the vegetable oil. Sauté the onions and mushrooms, remove them without draining the pan, and set aside on a plate.

3 In the same pan brown the meat in the remaining vegetable oil. Add the tomato paste and paprika. Add the onions and mushrooms back to the pan and stir. Remove the pan from the heat, add the sour cream, and stir.

4 Cook the noodles according to the package directions and drain. Don't stir the noodles and stroganoff together.

5 Divide the warm noodles among plates and ladle the desired amount of stroganoff on top of each serving of warm noodles. Sprinkle the parsley on top and serve.

MAKES 4 TO 6 SERVINGS.

COMPANY CASSEROLE

ELIZABETH REYNOLDS (Nashville, Tennessee) shares that Mimi, **PATRICIA ANN "PAT" ALLEY** (Brentwood, Tennessee), always makes sure we have the best home cooking for each and every meal. Elizabeth says, "When we were babies, she helped Mommy make our food using fresh vegetables from local farmers, steaming, food processing, and freezing them so Mommy's freezer was packed with green, orange, and yellow ice cubes."

---

1 pound ground beef

1/2 large green bell pepper, diced

1/4 medium onion, chopped

3 cans (8 ounces each) tomato sauce

1/2 package (8 ounces) extra-wide egg noodles

1 package (8 ounces) cream cheese, softened

1 container (8 ounces) cottage cheese

1 container (8 ounces) sour cream

---

1 Preheat the oven to 350 degrees.

2 In a large skillet brown the ground beef with the pepper and onion. Drain and return to the pan. Add the tomato sauce and mix well. Cover and simmer on low heat for 15 minutes.

3 Cook the noodles according to the package directions and drain.

4 In a small bowl mix the cream cheese, cottage cheese, and sour cream.

5 Spread the cheese mixture on the bottom of a 13 x 9-inch casserole dish. Top with the noodles and pour the meat and sauce mixture on top.

6 Bake uncovered for 30 minutes or until heated through. Serve warm.

MAKES 8 TO 10 SERVINGS.

DIXIE MEAT LOAF ✤✤✤

DANA BALLOU (Nashville, Tennessee) says that her Gran, NORMA RODGERS (Tullahoma, Tennessee), loved to watch her "'stories"—*As the World Turns* and *General Hospital*. Dana recalls, "When JFK was shot, the news coverage was all-day for about four days. Gran just fussed and fussed about not being able to see her stories. I asked her why she was so upset, and she said she was worried about one of the characters, who was having surgery just when her husband was about to leave her. She really thought those people were real! She also loved to watch the birds outside the den window from her rocking chair. She would talk to them and say, 'Hey, Tweetie.'"

2 pounds ground chuck

1 can (8 ounces) tomato sauce

1 medium onion, chopped

2 large eggs

pinch of salt

pinch of black pepper

1/4 teaspoon parsley

20 small saltine crackers, crumbled

1/4 cup milk

1/2 cup ketchup

1/2 medium green bell pepper, sliced into rings

1 Preheat the oven to 350 degrees.
2 In a large bowl mix the beef, tomato sauce, onion, eggs, salt, pepper, parsley, crackers, and milk. Shape the mixture into a loaf and place in a 2-quart casserole dish.
3 Cover and bake for 1 hour and 15 minutes. During the last 20 minutes of baking, uncover and brush the top of the meat loaf with the ketchup and top with the green pepper rings. Meat loaf is done when the center is no longer pink.

MAKES 6 SERVINGS.

NOTE: If you have picky eaters in your house, make mini meat loaves (as seen) with everyone's favorite ingredients.

OLD-FASHIONED POT ROAST

MARA BELL SIMPSON (Lebanon, Tennessee) was known to her grandchildren as Mamma May. "Mamma May was a great cook," says granddaughter **TERRI SIMPSON** (Nashville, Tennessee). "She used to keep a jar of bacon grease by the stove for cooking. A lot of people did this in the South, and some, of course, continue the practice. For her biscuits she used lard—not exactly heart healthy. Some of our other favorite things she made around the holidays were her homemade fudge and boiled custard."

MEAT:

½ cup all-purpose flour	5 pounds beef chuck roast, trimmed	5 bay leaves
½ teaspoon salt	¼ cup vegetable oil	⅛ teaspoon dried thyme
½ teaspoon black pepper	1 large onion, coarsely chopped	2 cups water
		1 cup coffee

GRAVY:

2 ½ cups water	2 tablespoons butter	½ cup whiskey

1 Preheat the oven to 325 degrees.
2 **TO PREPARE THE MEAT**, combine the flour, salt, and pepper on a large platter. Dust the beef roast with the seasoned flour, tapping off any excess flour. (Save the flour left on the platter to use in the gravy.)
3 Heat the oil in a large ovenproof skillet over medium heat. Add the roast and brown the meat on all sides, about 5 minutes per side. Remove the roast from the skillet.
4 Add the onion to the drippings in the skillet and sauté over medium heat until softened. Return the roast to the skillet and add the bay leaves, thyme, water, and coffee. Bring to a simmer for 20 minutes, stirring the liquid and turning the roast to combine the seasonings with the roast.
5 Cover the skillet and bake for 3 hours, or until fork-tender. Remove the roast from the skillet, discard any bones or gristle, cover loosely with aluminum foil, and set aside.

6 **TO PREPARE THE GRAVY**, place the skillet over medium heat and skim off any excess fat. Sprinkle the flour you dusted the meat with over the gravy in the skillet and cook for about 5 minutes, stirring until smooth and thickened. Add more water as needed to make the mixture a gravy consistency. Stir in the butter and whiskey.

7 Return the roast to the skillet with the gravy and heat through. Serve with potatoes, rice, or pasta, if desired.

MAKES 8 SERVINGS.

STEAK AND PAN GRAVY

MawMaw's response to any good thing is "Oh shoot!" share **FAITH AND SARAH JONES** (Thompson's Station, Tennessee). MawMaw, **BEVERLY DAVIS** (Brentwood, Tennessee), always has something good to eat at her house. Paw is convinced she is trying to kill him because she is such an amazing cook. He is always in trouble with the doctor for gaining weight and he always blames her.

2 to 3 cups self-rising flour

I teaspoon salt

I teaspoon black pepper

2 pounds beef cube steak, cut into bite-size pieces

1/4 cup vegetable oil

1/2 cup water

1 Mix the flour, salt, and pepper in a large Ziploc bag. Place the steak in the bag and shake to coat.

2 Heat the oil in a skillet. When the oil is hot, add the steak and brown on both sides. Reduce the heat, sprinkle in the flour mixture from the Ziploc bag over the top of the steak, and add the water. Mix together, cover, and simmer for 30 minutes. Add more water if needed. Serve the steak with the pan gravy.

MAKES 6 SERVINGS.

CREAMED CHICKEN ON CORNBREAD

"These biscuits are so thin, they squatted to rise." is a memorable quote that **KELLY SIMS** (Franklin, Tennessee) recalls from her Granny, **IRENE FOSTER** (Charlotte, Tennessee). Another one that makes her smile is, "This knife is so dull I could ride it to the mill." Kelly also shares that once when making a pound cake the top was overly browned, so Granny scraped off the "burnt" part with a knife and used a vacuum cleaner to remove the crumbs.

CREAMED CHICKEN:

1/2 stick butter

2 tablespoons minced celery

1 tablespoon minced onion

4 tablespoons all-purpose flour

2 cups chicken broth

1 cup heavy cream

1/2 teaspoon salt

1/4 teaspoon black pepper

4 cups diced cooked chicken

CORNBREAD:

1 stick butter

1/2 cup self-rising flour

1/2 cup self-rising cornmeal

2 large eggs, beaten

1/2 cup buttermilk

---

1 **TO MAKE THE CREAMED CHICKEN**, melt the butter in a large saucepan over medium-high heat. Sauté the celery and onion for 3 minutes. Add the flour and stir for 1 minute. Add the broth, cream, salt, and pepper and bring to a boil. Cook, stirring constantly, until the mixture thickens, about 4 minutes. Add the chicken. Simmer until heated. Remove from stove

2 **TO MAKE THE CORNBREAD**, preheat the oven to 400 degrees. Place the butter in an 8-inch round cast-iron skillet and place in the oven until melted. Remove from the oven (do not allow the butter to brown).

3 In a medium bowl combine the flour, cornmeal, eggs, and buttermilk. Add the melted butter and stir until all the ingredients are thoroughly combined. Pour the mixture into the hot cast-iron skillet.

4 Bake for 20 minutes, or until lightly browned. To serve, slice the cornbread into 8 slices and cover with the hot creamed chicken.

MAKES 8 SERVINGS.

CORENE'S HERB DUMPLINGS AND CHICKEN

J. Marie Hegler (Mount Juliet, Tennessee) shares that her grandmother, **Corene Botts Hegler Kolman** (Montgomery, Alabama), is loving and funny and reads more than anyone she knows, including herself. Marie says, "Her bookshelves are literally packed to overflowing. When the reading bug bit me, I used to go visit her and take an extra duffel bag to bring back a load of books to read (it was sometimes full with all of the books I was returning to her). It was nice to have that common bond and it was great having my own 'collection' from Grandmother's library. This dumpling recipe is very different from the traditional Southern version of this dish. These dumplings are not doughy and they have a lot of flavor from the herbs in them. They remind me a lot of the round German dumplings called knödel, which makes sense because of my family's German heritage, which is something common to many Southerners."

CHICKEN AND BROTH:

I fryer chicken, cut up, cooked in broth

1/2 cup water

1/4 cup all-purpose flour

DUMPLINGS:

1 1/2 cups all-purpose flour

2 teaspoons baking powder

3/4 teaspoon salt

1/8 teaspoon dried sage

1 tablespoon dried parsley

3/4 cup milk

1 **To make the chicken and broth**, place the chicken fryer pieces in a large pot or Dutch oven and cover with water. Bring to a boil, turn down to a simmer, and cook until the chicken falls off the bone, approximately 45 minutes. Pour the broth into a separate container. When the broth is cool, debone the chicken. Strain the broth back into the pot and bring back to a boil. In a small bowl whisk together the water and flour. Stir the flour mixture into the broth to thicken. Add the chicken meat back to the pot of broth and simmer on medium heat for 30 minutes.

2 **To make the dumplings**, in a medium bowl sift together the flour, baking powder, and salt. Mix in the sage and parsley. Once the broth is ready, pour the milk into the flour mixture and mix until blended (the batter will still be lumpy).

3 Using a spoon, drop the dumpling dough in 6 to 8 portions into the pot with the chicken and broth. Cook uncovered for 10 minutes. Cover the pot and cook for an additional 10 minutes. Serve hot.

MAKES 6 TO 8 SERVINGS.

BOTTS'S BRUNSWICK STEW

SHELLI HEGLER (Lowrenceville, Georgia) shares that every Christmas Eve her family gathered together at the home of her great-grandmother, **ROSA MAE LONG BOTTS** (Banks, Alabama), for the annual Christmas barbecue. Shelli says, "While the men slow-cooked the Boston butts over hickory coals just outside the field barn, the women would be getting the Brunswick stew, side dishes, and desserts ready for 'the feast' that took place around two o'clock. As kids, we spent our time going back and forth between the barbecue pit and the kitchen, trying to sneak tastes of all the delicious dishes. After everyone had eaten and we had opened gifts from whoever drew our name that year, we all went out into the field and shot off fireworks. My parents have taken over the tradition of hosting the annual Christmas barbecue and the guests have expanded to include any family and friends who can join us."

2 cups pulled, chopped chicken

2 cups pulled pork

2 onions, chopped

2 cans (15.25 ounces each) corn

2 cups cooked okra

2 cans (14.5 ounces each) diced tomatoes

2 cups cooked lima beans

I stick butter

3 cups chicken broth

I teaspoon Tabasco sauce (optional)

1/8 teaspoon salt

1/8 teaspoon black pepper

1 In a large heavy saucepan or Dutch oven, combine the chicken, pork, onions, corn, okra, tomatoes, lima beans, butter, broth, Tabasco sauce (if desired), salt, and pepper. Cook over low heat, stirring frequently to prevent scorching, until the stew is thick enough to eat with a fork, about 2 hours.

MAKES 10 TO 12 SERVINGS.

GRANNY D'S CHICKEN CASSEROLE

GWEN DEDRICK MCCOY (Hermitage, Tennessee) says that her Granny, **ALICE MAY DOWNEY** (Mobile, Alabama), had the most hilarious laugh. "It was more like a cackle, but you couldn't help but laugh too when you heard it," Gwen says. "Thinking about her cooking makes me miss her even more. There are so many great things she cooked, but I didn't ask her to write more recipes down for me—I wish I had."

6 boneless, skinless chicken breasts

1/4 teaspoon salt

2 tablespoons vegetable oil

2 1/2 cups chopped celery

2 cups chopped onions

5 large eggs, hard-boiled and chopped

1 cup mayonnaise

1 can (10.75 ounces) cream of chicken soup

1 can (10.75 ounces) cream of celery soup

1/4 teaspoon black pepper

1 sleeve saltine crackers, crushed

1 Preheat the oven to 350 degrees.

2 Place the chicken and salt in a large pot. Add water to cover the chicken and boil until the chicken is cooked, about 15 minutes. Drain, saving the broth in case you need to add it to the final mixture. Allow the chicken to cool.

3 Heat the oil in a medium skillet. Sauté the celery and onions for about 7 minutes and drain.

4 In a large bowl, combine the chicken, celery, onions, eggs, mayonnaise, cream of chicken soup, celery soup, and pepper.

5 Place the casserole mixture in 13 x 9-inch baking pan. Top with the crushed saltine crackers.

6 Bake for about 30 minutes, until bubbly and heated well through.

MAKES 6 TO 8 SERVINGS.

CHICKEN PUFFS ❈ ❈ ❈

Nana is what **KRISTEN VASGAARD** (Nashville, Tennessee), calls her grandma, **BETTY VASGAARD** (Knoxville, Tennessee). Kristen recalls that Nana had a number of memorable sayings. "Lord, ain't the gravy good" is a special favorite. Kristen says, "Nana would say that to indicate the rest of the meal may not have turned out well, but not to worry, because there was always something good on the table." After she passed away the family put together a cookbook of her best-loved recipes for her relatives, but they've since given hundreds of copies to friends and strangers who've requested the book as well.

---

1 package (3 ounces) cream cheese, softened

3 tablespoons butter, softened, divided

2 cups cubed cooked chicken

2 tablespoons milk

1/4 teaspoon salt

1/4 teaspoon black pepper

1 tablespoon chopped onion

1 tablespoon chopped pimientos

1 can (8 ounces) crescent rolls

1/2 cup dry seasoned bread crumbs

---

1 Preheat the oven to 350 degrees.
2 In a large bowl blend the cream cheese and 2 tablespoons of the softened butter. Add the chicken, milk, salt, pepper, onion, and pimientos and mix well.
3 Separate the crescent rolls into rectangles and place on an ungreased cookie sheet. Spoon 1/2 cup of the chicken mixture into the center of each rectangle. Pull up each corner to the center and twist to seal.
4 Melt the remaining 1 tablespoon butter and brush the tops of the chicken puffs with the butter. Sprinkle with the bread crumbs.
5 Bake for 20 to 25 minutes, until golden brown. Serve warm.

MAKES 6 SERVINGS.

NOTE: *If desired, top with a sauce made from heating half a can cream of mushroom soup mixed with milk.*

MAMA GRACE'S CHICKEN 'N' DUMPLINS

JAMIE ROBERTS (Nashville, Tennessee) shares that her Mama Grace, **GRACE MILLER COX**, was born in the tiny town of Millport, Alabama, but lived most of her life in Birmingham. Jamie says, "Mama Grace often cooked Sunday dinners for our family after church, but it was an extra-special day when we were served her chicken 'n' dumplins. Mama Grace cooked the dish with what seemed like very little effort—it wasn't until I asked my mom for the recipe that I realized just how careful you have to be, how important it is for a newbie to follow all the steps carefully. Yet, maybe because Mama Grace had rolled out the dough so many times after memorizing the recipe passed down from her own mother's voice, it became second nature to her. She served her chicken 'n' dumplins with cornbread, fresh tomatoes, and turnip greens from her garden, and the sweetest of sweet tea. 'No room for dessert, Mama,' you would protest feebly. 'Oh, surely you have room for chocolate pie,' she'd reply as she dished you out a slice."

CHICKEN:
1 whole chicken
   (3 pounds)

DUMPLINGS:

I large egg	1/2 teaspoon salt	I cup all-purpose flour
I tablespoon cold water	I teaspoon butter, melted	

BROTH:

4 cups chicken broth, from the cooked chicken	1/4 teaspoon white pepper	Cornstarch for thickening (optional)

1 **TO MAKE THE CHICKEN**, cover the chicken with water in a large pot and boil for I 1/2 hours. Remove the chicken from the water, cool, and take the chicken off the bone. Reserve the broth.

2 **To make the dumplings**, combine the egg, cold water, salt, butter, and flour in a medium bowl. Mix until the dough is thick and form the dough into a ball. Cover the bowl and let it sit in the refrigerator for 30 minutes. After the dough has "rested," place it on a lightly floured work surface and knead it. Roll out the dough until it is very thin. Cut it into 1 x 4-inch strips.

3 **To make the broth**, add the chicken broth and pepper to a large pot. Bring the broth to a rolling boil.

4 Slowly lower each dough strip into the broth. Keep the broth at a high boil to prevent the dough from sticking to the sides of the pot. When dumplings rise to the top, reduce the heat and simmer for 30 minutes. If the broth is not thick enough, add a little cornstarch. Divide the prepared chicken into six serving bowls. Ladle the dumplings and broth into each bowl and serve hot.

MAKES 6 SERVINGS.

BROCCOLI-CHICKEN CASSEROLE

ASHLEE CHANDLER's (Chattanooga, Tennessee) grandmother, SARA FAY WASSON SNOW (also of Chattanooga), was such a classy, sophisticated lady. "I had to look my best when I saw her because she was always in the best clothes and beautifully groomed," Ashlee says. "She read fashion magazines and watched television to know what was 'in.' I always thought this was neat since she was in her eighties and I was in my twenties—I had no idea what the latest trends were, but she did!"

1 pound boneless, skinless chicken breasts

2 packages (10 ounces each) frozen chopped broccoli, thawed

1 can (10.75 ounces) cream of chicken soup

1 can (10.75 ounces) cream of mushroom soup

2 cups shredded Cheddar cheese

1 cup mayonnaise

1 small onion, chopped

1 large egg, beaten

1 box (12 ounces) Ritz crackers

1 box (10 ounces) stuffing mix

1 Preheat the oven to 350 degrees.
2 In a large pot boil the chicken in water for 20 to 30 minutes. Drain and cool. Cut the chicken into cubes.
3 Cook the broccoli according to the package directions and drain.
4 In a large bowl mix the cream of chicken soup, cream of mushroom soup, cheese, mayonnaise, onion, and egg. Add the broccoli and mix well.
5 Cover the bottom of a lightly greased 13 x 9-inch casserole dish with the Ritz crackers. Place the chicken cubes on top of the crackers. Spoon the broccoli mixture over the chicken. Sprinkle the stuffing on top.
6 Bake uncovered for 30 minutes until bubbly and heated well through. Serve hot.

MAKE 6 SERVINGS.

GRANDMOTHER'S DEEP-FAT-FRIED CHICKEN

"Having a meal at Grandmother's was always something I looked forward to, because she loved to cook, especially for her family," says **NATALIE WELLS** (Nashville, Tennessee) of her grandmother, **WILLENE WELLS** (Huntsville, Alabama). "I was always given a choice of where to eat on my birthday, and out of all the places in Huntsville, I always picked Grandmother's house and requested her deep-fat-fried chicken!"

6 boneless chicken breasts	vegetable oil for frying	I tablespoon salt
2 cups buttermilk	3 cups all-purpose flour	

1 Place the chicken breasts in a 13 x 9-inch baking pan and cover them with the buttermilk. Cover the dish and refrigerate the chicken for at least 3 hours.

2 When you are ready to fry the chicken, pour the oil into a large, deep saucepan. Preheat the oil to 350 degrees.

3 Mix the flour and salt in a shallow bowl. Remove the chicken breasts from the buttermilk, but do not discard the buttermilk. Dredge each chicken breast in the flour mixture, making sure each piece is fully coated. Dip each piece back into the buttermilk and recoat with the flour mixture.

4 Place the chicken in the hot oil, one piece at a time, making sure the pieces don't stick together. The pieces will probably turn themselves as they bubble in the oil. Fry until the coating is deep golden brown, 7 to 10 minutes. After 5 minutes, check for even browning and turn as needed. Drain on paper towels and transfer to a wire rack, or keep warm in the oven until you finish frying all the chicken pieces. Serve warm.

MAKES 6 SERVINGS.

TANGY BARBECUED CHICKEN

DANA BALLOU (Nashville, Tennessee) says that her Gran, **NORMA RODGERS**, lived with her family in Tullahoma, Tennessee, when she was in high school until Gran passed away during Dana's senior year. Dana recalls, "When she passed away, it was the Christmas season and our high school Christmas dance was the next night. While we didn't really want to go, my mom made my brother and me go anyway, saying that Gran would never want us to pass up a chance to dance. Of this chicken recipe, Gran would say 'It's so sour you might just as well suck a lemon, but I love it!'"

CHICKEN:
1 whole chicken*

BARBECUE SAUCE:
2 cups cider vinegar

1 stick butter

3 tablespoons Worcestershire sauce

1 teaspoon crushed red pepper flakes

1/2 cup water

2 tablespoons all-purpose flour

1 **TO PREPARE THE CHICKEN**, cut it into pieces (breasts, thighs, wings, legs).

2 **TO MAKE THE BARBECUE SAUCE**, bring the vinegar, butter, Worcestershire sauce, and red pepper flakes to a boil. Reduce the heat to medium and thicken the sauce with the water and flour. (Add more flour if needed to thicken further.)

3 Grill the chicken pieces over medium heat. Once the outsides are brown, dunk each piece into the barbecue sauce and continue to grill until the meat reaches 190 degrees. Turn the chicken frequently, dunking in sauce each time. If desired, serve with coleslaw, sliced tomatoes, and corn on the cob for a truly Southern meal.

MAKES 3 TO 4 SERVINGS.

* This recipe works best when the chicken is used bone in, skin on.

❈❈❈ CHICKEN POTPIE

"Well I'll swan!" was used by **Lucille Windham Cummings** (Ecru, Mississippi) as an exclamation of disbelief and amazement. However, if something was really remarkable, she changed "swan" to "swannee," shares **Tammy Algood** (Smyrna, Tennessee). Tammy called her grandma Mama, yet all of the older relatives called her Toad—when she was born, her daddy used to tell everyone, "Come and look at my little toad frog!" Tammy says, "My grandmother rarely purchased canned vegetables at the grocery store, but mixed vegetables were always in her pantry for this dish. This potpie would be on the dinner table within a few days of a big weekend chicken meal. I serve it under the same circumstances and give a wink to Mama for the easy dinner everyone loves!"

3 cups chopped cooked chicken

1 can (14.5 ounces) mixed vegetables, drained

1 can (10.75 ounces) cream of celery soup

1 cup chicken broth

1/4 teaspoon black pepper

1 cup self-rising flour

1 cup milk

1 stick unsalted butter, melted

1 Preheat the oven to 400 degrees.

2 Spoon the chicken and vegetables evenly over the bottom of a lightly greased shallow 2-quart casserole dish.

3 In a small bowl whisk together the soup, broth, and pepper until smooth. Pour evenly over the chicken and vegetables.

4 In a separate small bowl combine the flour, milk, and melted butter, stirring until smooth. Spoon the dough over the top of the sauce in the casserole dish.

5 Bake uncovered for 45 to 50 minutes, or until golden brown. Cool for 10 minutes on a wire rack before serving.

MAKES 6 SERVINGS.

CHICKEN-FRIED STEAK

Nana is what **ALISON WASKIEWICZ** (Spring Hill, Tennessee) calls her grandma, **RUBY GIBBON** (Kingsport, Tennessee). Alison says, "When someone sneezed, Nana would say, 'Scat there, tomcat, get your tail out of the gravy!' We have no clue what she meant, but it was silly and funny to us. Nana says I can cook like her, which is a huge compliment. She used to make sugar cookies every holiday with her cookie cutters. I was really touched when she gave me all of those cookie cutters when she had to move to assisted living."

I pound beef cube steak

I large egg, lightly beaten

2 cups buttermilk

I cup all-purpose flour

1/8 teaspoon seasoned salt

1/4 teaspoon black pepper

vegetable oil for frying

---

1 Pound the steak to tenderize it and cut it into four pieces.
2 Combine the egg and buttermilk in a shallow bowl. Soak the steak in the buttermilk mixture. On a plate combine the flour, seasoned salt, and pepper. Remove one piece of steak from the buttermilk mixture and dredge it in the flour mixture on both sides. Repeat the process for the remaining pieces of steak.
3 Heat a 1/2-inch layer of oil in a deep cast-iron skillet. Place the steaks in the pan and cook for about 5 minutes on each side, until golden brown. Drain on paper towels and serve with chicken gravy.

MAKES 4 SERVINGS.

CRAB CAKES ✾✾✾

Grandma is what **MARY CLEVER** (Yorktown, Virginia) called her mom's mom, **ALICE S. SOLES**. Alice was born and raised in Gloucester, Virginia. Mary shares that Grandma could not stand, so she did all her cooking sitting on a stool.

I pound claw or regular crabmeat

2 large eggs, beaten

1/4 cup chopped onion

1/2 cup saltine cracker crumbs

3 tablespoons mayonnaise

I tablespoon prepared mustard

1/4 teaspoon Worcestershire sauce

3 tablespoons butter

---

1 Remove any bits of shell from the crabmeat, but keep the meat in lumps.
2 In a large bowl, mix the eggs, onion, cracker crumbs, mayonnaise, mustard, and Worcestershire sauce. Add the crabmeat and combine, being careful not to break up the lumps of crab.
3 Shape the mixture into small cakes about 4 inches in diameter.
4 Melt the butter in a skillet over medium heat. Fry the crab cakes until brown on each side, 3 1/2 to 4 minutes. Serve hot.

MAKES 5 TO 6 SERVINGS.

NOTE: *Finely chopped green bell pepper may be added if desired.*

✹✹✹ SALMON CROQUETTES

Mama, **LUCILLE WINDHAM CUMMINGS** (Ecru, Mississippi), had a big wooden bowl that was used for biscuit and bread dough making, shares **TAMMY ALGOOD** (Smyrna, Tennessee). "She stored it under the sink and it held her wooden rolling pin and was covered by a wooden cutting board that she used to roll the dough out on," Tammy says. "I can just see her hands working the dough and mixing together goodness in that bowl. I have her emerald ring that she always wore on her right hand and I never take it off. Sometimes when I look down and see my own hands mixing dough, I smile because it is a snapshot of her and how much love she managed to put into everything she made and did. I'm sure Mama used this recipe thanks to inexpensive canned salmon, but it was a regular entrée because we all loved it. I have the platter she used to serve these on and they just wouldn't taste the same coming to the table on anything else. I now serve them with cocktail sauce, but as a child, I only used ketchup."

vegetable oil or shortening for frying

1 can (14.75 ounces) pink salmon, drained

2 large eggs, lightly beaten

1/4 cup chopped onion

1/4 cup dry bread crumbs or all-purpose flour

2 tablespoons cornmeal

1/2 teaspoon salt

1/2 teaspoon black pepper

1 Place 1/2 inch of oil in a deep cast-iron skillet and place over medium-high heat.
2 Meanwhile, in a large bowl mix the salmon, eggs, onion, bread crumbs, cornmeal, salt, and pepper.
3 Form the mixture into 4 to 6 patties.
4 Place the patties in the preheated skillet and cook until both sides are golden brown, about 2 minutes per side. Drain on paper towels and serve warm.

MAKES 4 SERVINGS.

WELSH RAREBIT

Grandma **MILDRED GOODALL** is originally from Mount Juliet, Tennessee. Granddaughter **DAWN WRIGHT** (Hermitage, Tennessee) says Grandma loved to cook for her family and friends and to share her recipes. While it's claimed that Welsh rarebit hails from Great Britain, this cheese dish has been a standard in many Southern kitchens throughout the years. The word *rarebit* (as opposed to *rabbit*) lets tasters know the dish is meatless. Some say the difference is that Southern grandmas add a beaten egg and red pepper to theirs. One friend suggests adding chopped raw onion and dill or sweet pickles on top of the cheese sauce.

3 cups milk

3 cups grated sharp Cheddar cheese

3 heaping tablespoons all-purpose flour

1 tablespoon dry mustard

1/4 teaspoon ground cayenne pepper

2 tablespoons water

1 large egg

1 Combine the milk and cheese in a saucepan over low heat until the cheese is fully melted. Stir constantly so that the milk doesn't scorch. Remove from heat.

2 In a small bowl, mix the flour, mustard, cayenne pepper, and water. Combine to make a thin paste like a thin cake batter. Add the egg to the paste mixture and mix thoroughly. Ladle some of the hot milk and cheese mixture into the bowl to slowly heat the mixture. Add the contents of the bowl to the milk and cheese mixture in the saucepan.

3 Heat the rarebit over medium for 7 to 9 minutes, until it thickens to the consistency of Alfredo sauce. Serve hot over hot toast, or for an appetizer, pour over saltine crackers and top with lots of paprika.

MAKES 6 SERVINGS.

MISS CLARA'S SHRIMP GUMBO

Granny, **Clara Louise Suarez Plylar** (Biloxi, Mississippi), had a larger-than-life personality and a huge heart, according to granddaughter **Sharonda Hampton** (Mount Juliet, Tennessee). "She raised eight children on a fisherman's wage and fed them all very well," Sharonda says. "All of our family gatherings centered around food—and Granny usually provided the main dish. More times than not, it was her gumbo. Granny's gumbo was our traditional Christmas Eve dinner. The families would bring sides and sweets—but it was really the gumbo everyone was there for. Every Christmas Eve that I can remember, we met at her house until the house just got too small to hold all of us. Then we moved it to some of the children and grandchildren's homes. We kept that tradition going until my Granny passed away in 2006." Granny had many funny sayings, but most couldn't be reprinted here. One of her favorites was "I'm so hungry I see a bow-legged biscuit walking down cornbread lane."

---

2 pounds okra, cut in ½-inch rounds

2 cups distilled white vinegar

1 ¼ cups shortening, melted

1 ½ cups self-rising flour

1 ½ cups water

4 pounds smoked sausage, cut into bite-size pieces

3 pounds beef salami, cut into bite-size pieces

3 pounds ham, cut into bite-size pieces

1 bunch celery, chopped

3 large onions, chopped

4 large red or green bell peppers, cut into bite-size pieces

2 cans (28 ounces each) stewed tomatoes

10 pounds shrimp, washed and peeled

4 tablespoons gumbo filé*

---

1 Put the okra in a large bowl and cover with the vinegar. Let it sit for 5 minutes, but not longer. Drain the okra and rinse well.

---

* Gumbo filé is a spice used to season and thicken gumbo; it's made from dried and ground sassafras leaves.

2 To prepare a roux, melt the shortening in a heavy 2 1/2-gallon gumbo pot or a Dutch oven. Gradually add the flour, cooking over low heat. Cook, stirring continuously, until the roux is a dark nutty-brown color. Be careful not to allow the roux to scorch or burn (if the roux burns, you must start over). After browning, add the water and continue to cook until smooth.

3 Add the sausage, salami, and ham to the gumbo pot. Add enough water to allow the mixture to boil freely. Bring to a full boil, reduce the heat to low, and simmer for 20 minutes. Add the celery, onions, and bell peppers and continue cooking on low for an additional 20 minutes. Add the tomatoes and shrimp and continue cooking on low for 2 minutes. Add the prepared okra and the gumbo filé and continue cooking on low for about 15 minutes, until the shrimp are pink and the okra is done. Serve warm. If desired, serve on top of cooked rice.

MAKES ABOUT 2 TO 3 GALLONS.

Peach Cream Pie (page 175)

Pies and Cobblers

Mamaw's Pumpkin Pie
Raisin Pie
Ms. Rosa Mae's Sweet Potato Pie
Nana's Peach Cobbler
Mama Kee's Chess Pie
Peach Cream Pie
Fruit Cobbler
Coconut Pie
Blackberry Fried Pies
Southern Pecan Pie
Lemon Mist Pie

MAMAW'S PUMPKIN PIE

JEANNIE HIGGINS (Greeneville, Tennessee) shares that Mamaw, MARGARET HIPPS RICKER (Madison County, North Carolina), would always quote (even later in life when she had Alzheimer's), "I'm a Tar Heel born and a Tar Heel bred and when I die I'll be a Tar Heel dead." (North Carolina is known as the Tar Heel State, so many North Carolinians refer to themselves as Tar Heels.) This pumpkin pie is Jeannie's son Chris's absolute favorite pie in the world!

3 cups coarsely chopped fresh pumpkin

1 cup firmly packed brown sugar

3 large eggs, beaten

2 tablespoons butter, melted

2 tablespoons all-purpose flour

1 can (12 ounces) evaporated milk

1/4 teaspoon ground cinnamon

1/4 teaspoon ground nutmeg

1 pie crust (9 inches), unbaked

1 Preheat the oven to 450 degrees.
2 Cook the fresh pumpkin until all of the water is cooked out. Drain off any excess water and beat the pumpkin like mashed potatoes in a large bowl.
3 Add the brown sugar, eggs, melted butter, flour, milk, cinnamon, and nutmeg and beat until well combined. Pour the mixture into the pie crust.
4 Bake for 15 minutes. Reduce the temperature to 325 degrees and continue baking for another 45 to 60 minutes, or until a toothpick inserted in the center comes out clean. Cool on a wire rack for 45 to 60 minutes before slicing.

MAKES 6 SERVINGS.

NOTE: *There are many varieties of pumpkin and some make better pies than others—"pie pumpkins" are best. Once you remove the pumpkin seeds and "goop" you can cook the pumpkin on the stove, microwave, or bake it in the oven. If the pumpkin is cooked enough it should separate easily in large chucks and scoop easily out of the skin.*

RAISIN PIE ❖❖❖

MARY ANN MONK (Chuckey, Tennessee) shares that Mamaw, **MARGARET HIPPS RICKER** (Greeneville, Tennessee), loved to cook, bake, freeze, and can. Mary Ann recalls, "Sometimes when Mamaw made biscuits, the grandkids would watch and try to sneak a piece of dough to eat. Mamaw would give up a few pieces but also say, 'Getcha a cat head' or 'Getcha some Tommy toes,' which were small salad tomatoes."

2 cups raisins

2 cups water

1/2 cup firmly packed brown sugar

2 tablespoons cornstarch

1/2 teaspoon ground cinnamon

1/4 teaspoon salt

1 tablespoon distilled white vinegar

1 tablespoon butter

2 pie crusts (9 inches each), unbaked

1 Preheat the oven to 425 degrees.

2 Combine the raisins and water in a medium saucepan and boil for 5 minutes.

3 In a small bowl blend the brown sugar, cornstarch, cinnamon, and salt. Add to the raisin mixture and cook over medium heat, stirring until clear. Remove from the heat and stir in the vinegar and butter. Cool slightly.

4 Pour the mixture into one of the pie crusts. Cover the top of the pie with the other pie crust and cool the edges with your thumbs. Bake for about 30 minutes, or until golden brown. Cool 40 minutes on a wire rack before slicing.

MAKES 6 TO 8 SERVINGS.

MS. ROSA MAE'S SWEET POTATO PIE

J. MARIE HEGLER (Mount Juliet, Tennessee) shares that her great-grandmother, **ROSA MAE LONG BOTTS** (Banks, Alabama), could produce the most amazing food—just good country cookin'—out of the small kitchen in her house on the family farm. While both Grandma and the family farm are gone now, the memories and the recipes will last forever.

2 1/2 cups sugar

1 3/4 sticks margarine

2 large eggs

1 1/2 teaspoons vanilla extract

1 1/2 teaspoons lemon or orange extract

3 cups mashed sweet potatoes

2 pie crusts (9 inches each), unbaked

1 Preheat the oven to 450 degrees.

2 In a large bowl cream together the sugar and margarine. Add the eggs, one at a time, followed by the vanilla and lemon or orange extract. Mix in the mashed sweet potatoes, 1 cup at a time. Mix until very smooth and then pour into the 2 pie crusts.

3 Bake for 10 minutes. Reduce the temperature to 350 degrees and continue baking for another 35 to 45 minutes, or until a toothpick inserted in the center comes out clean. Cool on a wire rack for 45 to 60 minutes before slicing.

MAKES 2 PIES.

NANA'S PEACH COBBLER

MARY ANN LAWSON (Nashville, Tennessee) shares that her Nana, **VENICE WILSON** (Mayfield, Kentucky), was a wonderful cook. "I would pull my chair up to the kitchen counter right next to her and I would watch her do her thing," Mary Ann recalls. "She always let me help make desserts—that's how I learned to make this special peach cobbler. I'm fortunate that she passed down many of her wonderful recipes to both my mother and me."

FILLING:

3 cups peeled and
   sliced peaches

I tablespoon lemon
   juice

1/2 cup sugar

2 tablespoons
   cornstarch

1/4 teaspoon almond
   extract

TOPPING:

I cup all-purpose
   flour

I cup sugar

I teaspoon salt

I large egg, beaten

I stick butter

1 Preheat the oven to 350 degrees.

2 **TO MAKE THE FILLING**, combine the peaches, lemon juice, sugar, cornstarch, and almond extract in a medium bowl. Mix well and spoon into a 9-inch square baking pan.

3 **TO MAKE THE TOPPING**, combine the flour, sugar, salt, and egg in a medium bowl. With a fork or pastry cutter, work in the butter until crumbly. Spoon the topping on top of the peaches.

4 Bake for 45 minutes, or until lightly browned on top. Serve warm or cool.

MAKES 5 TO 6 SERVINGS.

MAMA KEE'S CHESS PIE

EDITH McKEE was born in Murfreesboro, Tennessee, but lived most of her adult life in Nashville. Her last name was McKee, so she was affectionately known as Mama Kee. She was a great cook and gardener and loved animals. Granddaughter **KAY STROM** (Nashville, Tennessee) recalls that Mama Kee was also an excellent seamstress. Kay shares that every spring they would go to the fabric store to pick out a pattern for her Easter dress. "Almost every time I tried one on for a fitting I would get stuck by at least one straight pin, because she always forgot to take them all out," says Kay.

I 3/4 cups sugar

I tablespoon all-purpose flour

I tablespoon cornmeal

3/4 cup margarine, melted

3 large eggs

I can (12 ounces) evaporated milk

I teaspoon vanilla

I pie crust (9 inches), unbaked

1 Preheat the oven to 350 degrees.

2 Mix the sugar, flour, and cornmeal in a medium bowl. Add the melted margarine and cream well. Beat in the eggs one at a time. Mix in the milk and vanilla. Pour into the pie crust.

3 Bake for 45 minutes until set and lightly brown on top.

MAKES 8 SERVINGS.

ADELE NAIFEH (Covington, Tennessee) is known as Sittie to her granddaughter, **SAMEERA LOW** (Brentwood, Tennessee). *Sittie* means "grandmother" in Arabic—the family is part Lebanese. Sameera says, "Sittie didn't care how the pie looked when she cut a piece to put on a plate—the messier the better! She said our tummies wouldn't mind a bit, and they didn't! With a huge garden and an orchard full of apples, peaches, apricots, and plums, she was always making something yummy. This peach cream pie was her answer to whatever ailed you. I remember being sick with a fever and lying in bed, and Sittie brought over a peach cream pie to make me feel better. Whenever we get really good fresh peaches, my sister and I make the pie now as grown-ups—we love how it takes us right back to our childhood. And we think it really is the most delicious dessert in the world!"

PIE:

2/3 cup sugar

1/3 cup all-purpose flour

1/4 teaspoon salt

2 cups milk

2 large eggs, slightly beaten

1 teaspoon vanilla extract

1 pie crust (9 inches), baked

6 peaches, peeled and sliced

TOPPING:

1 1/2 cups heavy whipping cream

1/2 cup sugar

---

1 **TO MAKE THE PIE**, mix the sugar, flour, and salt in the top of a double boiler. Slowly add the milk. Cook in the double boiler over medium heat, stirring constantly, until thick. Gradually stir the eggs into the mixture. Continue cooking over medium heat for 5 minutes, stirring constantly. Add the vanilla and stir. Allow the mixture to cool. When cool, pour into the baked pie crust. Place the peaches on top of the mixture inside the pie crust.

2 **TO MAKE THE TOPPING**, use an electric mixer to whip the cream until stiff. Gradually add the sugar and continue to mix. Spoon the whipped cream on top of the pie. Chill in the refrigerator for at least 2 hours before serving.

MAKES 8 SERVINGS.

FRUIT COBBLER

JANET KEESE DAVIES (Nashville, Tennessee) says her grandmother, LUCY BEALL KEESE, was born and raised in Cuthbert, Georgia. "When she was quite elderly, my cousins took her back to her old hometown," Janet says. "She looked around and said, 'I have so many lovely memories here—if only I could remember them!'" Lucy passed away in 1959.

2 tablespoons butter

2/3 cup all-purpose flour

1 1/2 teaspoons baking powder

1/2 teaspoon salt

1/2 cup sugar

2/3 cup milk

3 cups sliced peaches or whole blueberries or blackberries

1 Preheat the oven to 350 degrees. Melt the butter in an 8-inch square baking pan in the oven.

2 In a small bowl mix the flour, baking powder, salt, sugar, and milk. Pour the batter over the butter. Top with the fruit.

3 Bake for 45 to 55 minutes, or until brown and bubbly. Serve warm plain or with ice cream, if desired.

MAKES 4 TO 6 SERVINGS.

KELLY AMOS (Pittsboro, North Carolina) shares that her Grandma Franklin, THELMA FRANKLIN (Chase City, Virginia), always had homemade desserts to share at both lunch and supper—often including this coconut pie. Kelly recalls, "When my grandfather was still working, he would take a slice for lunch. She also would give these away as Christmas presents in December."

1/2 stick butter

1 cup sugar

3/4 cup milk

3 large eggs

3/4 cup sweetened flaked coconut

1 pie crust (9 inches), unbaked

---

1 Preheat the oven to 325 degrees.

2 Melt the butter in a medium saucepan. Add the sugar and milk to the saucepan and heat through. Transfer to a medium bowl. Add the eggs and mix well. Add the coconut and continue to mix. Pour into the pie crust.

3 Bake for 25 to 35 minutes, or until the pie is firm. Allow to cool on a wire rack before slicing.

MAKES 6 TO 8 SERVINGS.

BLACKBERRY FRIED PIES

LEIGH ANDERSON (Nashville, Tennessee), shares that her Memi, JACQUELYN B. ANDERSON (also of Nashville), is a bit of an insomniac. Rather than reading or watching TV like most of the sleep-deprived population, when she awakens in the middle of the night, Memi Jackie bakes to pass the time. Also true to Southern culture, she possesses a knack for deftly gathering pieces of information, even when you think she's not listening. Mention in passing that you like blackberries and she may nod and offer a trademark "bless your heart." You'll forget you even mentioned anything about blackberries. But sure enough, by the next afternoon she will have stashed a plate of hot, fresh blackberry fried pies in your mailbox!

DOUGH:

2 cups all-purpose flour

1/4 teaspoon baking soda

1/4 teaspoon salt

1/2 cup vegetable oil

1/3 cup buttermilk

vegetable oil for frying

FILLING:

1/2 cup sugar

I tablespoon cornstarch

1/2 cup water

2 cups fresh or frozen blackberries

I tablespoon lemon juice

3/4 teaspoon ground cinnamon

Powdered sugar for dusting (optional)

1 TO MAKE THE DOUGH, combine the flour, baking soda, and salt in a large bowl. Combine the oil and buttermilk in a small bowl. Stir the buttermilk mixture into the flour mixture until the dough forms a ball.

2 Roll out the dough on a floured work surface to a 1/8-inch thickness. Cut the dough into ten 4 1/2-inch circles.

3 TO MAKE THE FILLING, combine the sugar, cornstarch, and water in a saucepan. Add the blackberries, lemon juice, and cinnamon. Cook over medium heat, stirring frequently, until the mixture comes to a boil. Cook and stir for an additional 2 to 3 minutes. Remove from the heat and cool.

4 Place I tablespoon of the blackberry mixture on one-half of each dough circle. Fold over into a half circle, sealing the edges closed with a fork.

5 Add $1/4$ to $1/2$ inch of oil to a deep skillet. Over medium heat, fry the pies until they are golden brown, about $1^{1}/2$ minutes per side. Drain on paper towels. If desired, dust with powdered sugar before serving. Serve warm or at room temperature.

MAKES 9 TO 10 PIES.

SOUTHERN PECAN PIE

Grandma **ERMA SMITH** (Tupelo, Mississippi) made the best pecan pie, shares grand-daughter-in-law **FAYE MCGEE** (Nashville, Tennessee). Aunt Sarah Smith carries on the tradition of making the best pecan pie these days. Faye's husband, Terry, often spent the summers with his Southern grandparents. As his grandfather came in through the back-door and called out to his wife, his Southern drawl sounded as if he were calling her "Hammer." It would be years before Terry learned that his grandmother's real name was actually Erma.

3 large eggs

3/4 cup sugar

1 cup light corn syrup

2 tablespoons unsalted butter, softened

1 heaping tablespoon all-purpose flour

1 teaspoon vanilla extract

1 cup chopped pecans

1 pie crust (9 inches), unbaked

1 Preheat the oven to 350 degrees.

2 In a large bowl whisk together the eggs. Whisk in the sugar. Add the corn syrup and butter and mix well. Add the flour and vanilla and mix well. Add the pecans and stir until well moistened. Place the pie crust into an ungreased 9-inch pie pan. Pour the mixture into the pie crust.

3 Bake for 55 to 60 minutes, or until a toothpick inserted into the center comes out clean. About halfway through baking, cover the outside edges of the pie with foil to prevent overbrowning. Allow to cool on a wire rack for 45 minutes before slicing.

MAKES 6 TO 8 SERVINGS.

LEMON MIST PIE

LUANNE GREER (Dickson, Tennessee) called her grandma MaMaw, but the family spelled it "Mama." Mama was **LESSIE DORTCH ANDERSON**, who was born in Dover, Tennessee, and lived in Dickson, Tennessee. Luanne says, "Mama was the hardest-working person I have ever been around. She was a schoolteacher and put up during the summer almost all of the food they ate. She could make anything taste good. Mama was also a manners person and she had rules at the table. My granddaddy would always try to get me in trouble!"

3 large eggs yolks

1/2 cup plus 2 tablespoons sugar, divided

1/4 teaspoon salt

I tablespoon grated lemon rind

3 tablespoons lemon juice, unstrained

6 tablespoons boiling water

3 tablespoons lemon gelatin, unprepared

3 large egg whites

1/4 teaspoon cream of tartar

I pie crust (9 inches), baked

1 **TO MAKE THE FILLING**, beat the egg yolks with a spoon in the top of a double boiler. Stir in 5 tablespoons of the sugar, the salt, lemon rind, and lemon juice. Cook over boiling water, stirring, until the custard is thick enough to coat a metal spoon. This should take about 10 minutes.

2 In a medium bowl stir 6 tablespoons boiling water into the lemon gelatin. Beat the hot lemon custard into it with a whisk. Cool until the mixture begins to set, 25 to 45 minutes. Beat slightly to break it up. Let it stand while making the meringue.

3 **TO MAKE THE MERINGUE**, beat the egg whites with the cream of tartar with an electric mixer, until they are stiff and peaks form. Gradually add the remaining 5 tablespoons sugar, beating continually.

4 Carefully fold the meringue into the cooled custard. Spoon the folded mixture into the baked pie crust. Refrigerate until well chilled, about 2 hours.

MAKES 6 TO 8 SERVINGS.

NOTE: *This pie is also good with a vanilla-wafer crumb crust.*

Jam Layer Cake (page 188)

Cakes

Gooey Cake à la
Grandma H.

Speedy Spice Cake

Jam Layer Cake

Nanny's Coconut Cake

Rhubarb Crumb Cake

Memama's Chocolate
Sheet Cake

Rave-Review Cake

White Cake
with Caramel Icing

Red Velvet Cake

Orange-Slice Cake

Nanny's Lady
Baltimore Cake

Mamaw's Strawberry
Pudding Cake

Lizzie's Sour Cream
Pound Cake

Mema's Pecan
Bundt Cake

Mom's Gingerbread

Esther's Pumpkin Cake

Coca-Cola Cake

Esther's Apple Cake

GOOEY CAKE À LA GRANDMA H. ❈❈ ❈❈

CARSON BROWN (Franklin, Tennessee) shares that she and her grandma, **BRENDA HUDIBURG** (Nashville, Tennessee), have special matching aprons they always wear when they cook and bake together. Carson says, "After cooking we end up with flour or chocolate all over our hands, noses, and aprons—every time! When we sample some of our creations, Grandma always tells me, 'Don't forget to eat the orphans,' meaning the leftover drips or bites."

---

3 large eggs, divided

1 box (18.25 ounces) yellow cake mix

1 stick butter, melted

1 package (8 ounces) cream cheese, softened

1 package (16 ounces) powdered sugar

---

1 Preheat the oven to 350 degrees.

2 Beat 1 egg in a large bowl. Mix in the cake mix and the butter. Spread the batter into a lightly greased 13 x 9-inch baking pan, making a slightly raised edge around the pan.

3 In a medium bowl beat the remaining 2 eggs. Blend in the softened cream cheese. Gradually mix in the powdered sugar. Pour the mixture over the cake batter in the pan.

4 Bake for 35 to 40 minutes. The center should still be a bit gooey. Allow to cool before cutting or serving.

MAKES 8 TO 10 SERVINGS.

 **SPEEDY SPICE CAKE**

JEAN SMITH (Mooreville, Mississippi) called her grandmother Ma. Ma was **MILEY PETAGO GARNER** (Lee County, Mississippi). Jean says that her family still owns her grandparents' farm and home. Ma never worked outside her home—her business was keeping all of her six children happy and well fed. Jean learned a lot from Ma about cooking, baking, and canning. Ma taught her how to make pickles and she still uses many of her recipes. "Ma was the epitome of a grandmother, with her shiny brown eyes and fluffy white hair," Jean says. "She and my Pa grew gardens and she knew a lot about how to preserve and prepare good food and lots of it. She always had company to eat at her house. And when my sister and I were growing up, we liked to take our friends there as well. Ma was known for this spice cake—she made so many that her house actually smelled like the spices."

CAKE:
- 1/2 cup shortening
- 1 1/4 cups sugar
- 2 large eggs, unbeaten
- 3/4 cup milk
- 2 cups cake flour, sifted

- 2 teaspoons baking powder
- 3/4 teaspoon salt
- 1/2 teaspoon ground cinnamon
- 1/2 teaspoon ground cloves

- 1/2 teaspoon ground allspice
- 2 tablespoons molasses
- 1 teaspoon vanilla extract

TOPPING:
- 1/3 cup firmly packed brown sugar

- 1 tablespoon butter, melted
- 1 tablespoon water

- 1/3 cup chopped pecans (optional)

1 Preheat the oven to 350 degrees.
2 **TO MAKE THE CAKE,** in a large bowl cream together the shortening and sugar. Add the eggs and milk and beat well by hand until smooth. In a medium bowl combine the cake flour, baking powder, salt, cinnamon, cloves, and allspice. Add the flour mixture to the creamed mixture. Add the molasses and vanilla and mix well. Pour into a greased and floured 13 x 9-inch baking pan.

3 Bake for 35 to 40 minutes, or until a toothpick inserted in the center comes out clean. Frost immediately.

4 **TO MAKE THE TOPPING**, in a medium saucepan combine the brown sugar, melted butter, water, and pecans. Cook over medium heat until the ingredients have melted. Pour over the hot cake and serve warm.

MAKES 12 TO 14 SERVINGS.

JAM LAYER CAKE

BELINDA BASS (Nashville, Tennessee) called her grandma MamaJohn. **LAURA BELLE HILL** lived in Weir, Kentucky, where she was born and raised. "She wrote very few recipes down but was the best cook I have ever known," Belinda says. "MamaJohn made special cinnamon-sugar cookies that she called tea cakes, but unfortunately no recipe exists. She used to let me cut out biscuits with a pill bottle, as well as make every creature I could imagine with the raw dough and then eat them. I didn't taste a biscuit from a can until I was in college. MamaJohn was raised on well water and had poor dental care, so she lost her teeth early in life and had to wear dentures. To make us laugh, she would take out her teeth and sing hymns!"

CAKE:
- 2 cups jam*
- 3 sticks butter
- 2 cups sugar
- 6 large eggs, beaten
- I 1/2 cups buttermilk
- 4 1/2 cups self-rising flour
- 2 teaspoons ground cinnamon
- 2 teaspoons ground allspice
- 2 teaspoons ground cloves
- 2 teaspoons ground nutmeg
- 2 teaspoons baking soda
- I teaspoon cocoa

ICING:
- 2 1/2 cups sugar, divided
- 3/4 cup evaporated milk
- 1/8 teaspoon baking soda
- 2 tablespoons butter

1 Preheat the oven to 350 degrees.
2 **TO MAKE THE CAKE**, in a large bowl cream together the jam, butter, and sugar. Add the eggs, buttermilk, flour, cinnamon, allspice, cloves, nutmeg, baking soda, and cocoa and mix well. Pour the batter into 4 greased and floured 9-inch round cake pans.

* MamaJohn used blackberry jam that she put up herself.

3 Bake for 20 to 25 minutes, or until a toothpick inserted in the center comes out clean. Let the cakes cool before icing.

4 **To make the icing**, brown $1/2$ cup of the sugar in a skillet. Add the remaining 2 cups sugar, milk, baking soda, and butter and boil until the mixture reaches the soft-ball stage. (If you put a drop of the cooked mixture into a cup of cold water and it forms a soft ball, the mixture is ready.) Remove from the heat and let the icing cool. Beat with an electric mixer until it reaches spreading consistency. Spread the icing between each layer of the cake and then ice the top and sides.

MAKES 10 TO 12 SERVINGS.

❈❈❈ NANNY'S COCONUT CAKE

ANNA MAE JACKSON (Hermitage, Tennessee) was known as Nanny to granddaughter **ASHLEY LARMER** (Nashville, Tennessee). "Nanny's fresh coconut cake was legendary—while her applesauce and jam cakes were wonderful, her coconut cake was my favorite," Ashley says. "She would only make it at the holidays. Anyone who has made a fresh coconut cake knows that it is not a delicate process. I remember her whacking the coconut with a small hammer, shaking the countertops, the light fixtures, and the windows! We'd sit at the kitchen table and I would help her apply the shredded coconut to the outside of the cake, being careful to cover every inch. Nanny would hide the finished masterpiece with a shiny aluminum cake cover, and then it was sent to the back bedroom, which was always much cooler than the rest of the house. She would let it 'set' for a day or two before serving it. It was torture knowing that the delicious cake was back there, waiting to be eaten, but it was always worth the wait. Since she passed away, I make the coconut cake for our family at the holidays. While mine doesn't hold a candle to hers, I think she would be proud that I have carried on her tradition."

1 large ripe coconut

CAKE:

2 1/4 cups cake flour	1 teaspoon salt	1 teaspoon coconut extract
1 1/2 cups sugar	1/2 cup shortening	4 large egg whites
3 1/2 teaspoons baking powder	1 cup milk, divided	

SIMPLE SYRUP:

1 cup water	1 cup sugar	Reserved coconut milk

WHITE MOUNTAIN ICING:

1 cup sugar	1/2 cup light corn syrup	2 teaspoons vanilla extract
4 tablespoons water	4 large egg whites	

1 Preheat the oven to 350 degrees.

2 **TO PREPARE THE COCONUT**, using an awl and hammer, carefully poke holes in the "eyes" of the coconut. Strain the coconut milk over a measuring cup covered with several layers of cheesecloth. Hammer along the midline of the coconut very carefully, splitting it open into several large pieces. Use the awl to pry away the coconut shell. Peel the skin off the coconut using a sharp vegetable peeler or paring knife. Using the shredder attachment on your food processor, shred the coconut. Set the shredded coconut and coconut milk aside.

3 **TO MAKE THE CAKE**, sift together the flour, sugar, baking powder, and salt. Add the shortening, 2/3 cup of the milk, and the coconut extract. Beat for 2 minutes with an electric mixer. Add the remaining 1/3 cup milk and the egg whites. Beat 2 more minutes. Pour into 3 greased and generously floured 8-inch round cake pans.

4 Bake for 20 minutes, or until a toothpick inserted in the center comes out clean. Cool the cakes in the pans for 5 to 10 minutes and then transfer to wire racks to cool completely.

5 **TO MAKE THE SIMPLE SYRUP**, bring the water to a boil in a saucepan. Add the sugar and coconut milk and stir until dissolved. Remove from the heat and allow to cool.

6 **TO MAKE THE ICING**, mix the sugar, water, and corn syrup in a saucepan. Cover and cook until the mixture reaches 242 degrees, as measured with a candy thermometer. Just before the syrup is ready, beat the egg whites in the bowl of an electric mixer until stiff enough to hold a peak. While the mixer is running, pour the hot syrup very slowly in a thin stream into the beaten egg whites. Continue to beat until the icing holds peaks. Blend in the vanilla.

7 **TO ASSEMBLE THE CAKE**, poke holes in each layer and brush each layer with one-third of the simple syrup. Frost the bottom layer and spread a handful of coconut on top. Place the second layer on top and frost. Spread a handful of coconut on top and place the final layer on top. Frost the top and sides of the entire cake and cover completely with the remaining coconut. Keep in a cool room or refrigerate.

MAKES 10 TO 12 SERVINGS.

RHUBARB CRUMB CAKE

CHARLENE BOYCE (Nashville, Tennessee) didn't get to know her Gram until much later in life. When Gram, **DOROTHY C. JOHNSON**, fell in 2002, Charlene moved to Fremont, Nebraska, to make sure she was okay. After eighteen months, she moved Gram to Nashville to live with her for eight years before having to go to a nursing home. Gram tells stories about picking the rhubarb from her garden to make her cakes and crisps.

CAKE:

1 ½ cups firmly packed brown sugar

½ cup margarine

1 large egg

3 cups all-purpose flour

1 teaspoon baking soda

1 cup buttermilk

1 teaspoon vanilla extract

½ teaspoon salt

1 ½ cups diced rhubarb

TOPPING 1:

½ cup sugar

1 teaspoon ground cinnamon

OR TOPPING 2:

½ cup orange juice

½ cup firmly packed brown sugar

½ cup chopped walnuts

---

1 Preheat the oven to 350 degrees.

2 **TO MAKE THE CAKE**, in a large bowl mix together the brown sugar, margarine, egg, flour, baking soda, buttermilk, vanilla, salt, and rhubarb. Pour the batter into a greased 13 x 9-inch baking pan.

3 **TO MAKE TOPPING 1**, in a small bowl mix the sugar and cinnamon together and sprinkle over the batter.

4 **OR TO MAKE TOPPING 2**, in a small bowl mix the orange juice, brown sugar, and walnuts and sprinkle over the batter.

5 Cover and bake for 50 minutes, or until a toothpick inserted in the center comes out clean. Cool on a wire rack before serving.

MAKES 10 TO 12 SERVINGS.

MEMAMA'S CHOCOLATE SHEET CAKE

Memama, **DORRIS CURTIS HINSON** (Charlotte, Tennessee), said that this was "good cake and easy to make," shares **GRACE HINSON** (Cumberland Furnace, Tennessee). "Memama told us not to open the oven or the middle of the cake would sink, but we thought she was joking—she wasn't!" Grace says. "The last time I got to be with Memama was just before she passed away. She taught my cousin, Rachel, and me how to make this cake. It was delicious! That's a special memory I will always cherish. She also taught me to play the dulcimer a couple of years ago and we enjoyed playing together often."

CAKE:

2 sticks margarine

1/4 cup cocoa

1/2 cup buttermilk

2 cups sugar

2 cups all-purpose flour

I teaspoon baking soda

I teaspoon salt

1/2 cup water

I teaspoon vanilla extract

2 large eggs, slightly beaten

ICING:

I stick margarine

6 tablespoons buttermilk

1/4 cup cocoa

I package (16 ounces) powdered sugar

1 Preheat the oven to 350 degrees.

2 **TO MAKE THE CAKE**, melt the margarine in a 13 x 9-inch baking pan in the oven. Remove the pan and stir in the cocoa and buttermilk. In a large bowl mix the sugar, flour, baking soda, salt, water, and vanilla. Add the contents of the baking pan to the mixture in the bowl. Add the eggs and stir well. Pour the mixture back into the baking pan.

3 Bake for 30 to 40 minutes, or until a toothpick inserted into the center comes out clean. Allow to cool completely before frosting.

4 **TO MAKE THE ICING**, melt the margarine in a saucepan over low heat. Stir in the buttermilk and cocoa and bring to a bubbly boil. Gradually add the powdered sugar. Mix well and then pour over the cake.

MAKES 10 TO 12 SERVINGS.

Gigi is what **KELSEY COPELAND** (Mount Juliet, Tennessee) calls her grandma. Gigi is **BETTY COPELAND**, who was born in Livingston, Tennessee, and now lives in Hermitage. Kelsey says, "When I was little, I would go over to my grandmother's house to spend the night. One of our favorite things to do was have tea parties. We'd sit at a little table on the porch and eat grilled cheese and drink sweet tea. Such sweet memories!"

CAKE:

1 package (18.25 ounces) white or yellow cake mix

1 package (3 ounces) instant vanilla pudding

1 1/3 cups water

4 large eggs

1/4 cup vegetable oil

1 1/2 cups sweetened coconut flakes

1 cup chopped pecans

ICING:

1/3 cup butter

6 ounces cream cheese

1 package (16 ounces) powdered sugar

4 teaspoons milk

1/2 teaspoon vanilla extract

1 cup toasted coconut

1 Preheat the oven to 350 degrees.

2 **TO MAKE THE CAKE**, add the cake mix, pudding mix, water, eggs, and oil to the bowl of an electric mixer. Blend on medium speed for 4 minutes. Stir in the coconut flakes and pecans. Pour into a greased and floured 10-inch tube pan.

3 Bake for 60 minutes, or until a toothpick inserted in the center comes out clean. Cool for 15 minutes and remove the cake from the pan. Continue to cool on a wire rack.

4 **TO MAKE THE ICING**, in a medium bowl cream the butter and blend in the cream cheese. Add the powdered sugar alternately with the milk, beating well after each addition. Mix in the vanilla. Spread the icing over the top and sides of the cake. Sprinkle the toasted coconut over the icing. This cake is better if eaten the next day.

MAKES 10 TO 12 SERVINGS.

WHITE CAKE WITH CARAMEL ICING

Suga is what **WREN FRANKLIN** (Nashville, Tennessee) called her grandmother, **JAMA FRANKLIN**. Suga was born in Sevierville, Tennessee, and later lived in Gallatin. Wren shares that Suga used to say, "I don't know if the food is really this good or if I'm just hungry!" While she passed away in 1987, special memories for Wren include being amidst the hustle and bustle of the kitchen at Christmas with Grandmother, Aunt Irene, Lula Mae, and Lillie Bell. "This culinary dream team could cook any and every thing, and it was *all* good," Wren shares.

CAKE:

2 sticks butter

I cup sugar

3 cups all-purpose flour

3 teaspoons baking powder

1/4 teaspoon salt

I cup milk

8 large egg whites

I teaspoon vanilla extract

ICING:

3 1/2 cups sugar, divided

3/4 cup water

2 sticks butter

I cup heavy cream

1 Preheat the oven to 350 degrees.

2 **TO MAKE THE CAKE**, cream together the butter and sugar in a large bowl. Sift together the flour, baking powder, and salt in a medium bowl. Add the flour mixture alternately with the milk to the butter mixture, beating well after each addition. In a small bowl beat the egg whites until stiff. Fold the egg whites into the batter. Add the vanilla extract and mix well. Pour the batter into 3 wax paper–lined 9-inch round cake pans (place wax paper on the bottom and grease and flour the sides).

3 Bake for 25 to 30 minutes, or until a toothpick inserted in the center comes out clean. Cool cake completely before frosting.

4 **To make the icing**, brown or caramelize 1/2 cup of the sugar in a small cast iron skillet. To caramelize, place the sugar in an even layer on the bottom of the skillet. Cook on medium heat. Add the water to the sugar and stir constantly with a wooden spoon. Keep scraping down the sides of the skillet to keep the sugar cooking consistently. Stir the mixture until it reaches a boil. Swirl the pan around to keep the syrup moving until it begins to turn amber brown. Remove from the heat.

5 In a saucepan bring the remaining 3 cups sugar, the butter, and cream to a boil. Add the hot syrup mixture to the boiling butter mixture and cook on medium until the icing reaches the soft-ball stage. (If you put a drop of the cooked mixture into a cup of cold water and it forms a soft ball, the mixture is ready.) Cool for a few minutes. Transfer to the bowl of an electric mixer and beat for several minutes, until the icing is creamy and a spreadable consistency. If the icing gets too thick, add a little milk. To test the icing, try spreading it on the inside of the mixer bowl. Spread the icing between each layer of the cake and on the top and sides. If the icing needs a little more smoothing after it is on the cake, dip the spreading knife into warm water and smooth the icing, giving it a slick appearance.

MAKES 10 TO 12 SERVINGS.

Note: *This is a very moist cake and you can make it ahead of time and freeze, if desired. It is much easier to frost when frozen.*

RED VELVET CAKE

What **Georgia Thompson McGrew** (Nashville, Tennessee) remembers most about Grandma Hanny, **Hannah Eades** (Somerset, Kentucky), was that she walked with a crutch as the result of a car and train accident. Hanny was always in the kitchen with the other womenfolk and they were usually wearing aprons over their dresses. Georgia first tasted red velvet cake at age seven and has requested it for her birthday ever since.

CAKE:

1 1/2 cups sugar

1 1/4 sticks butter

3 large eggs

1 tablespoon distilled white vinegar

1 tablespoon cocoa

1 ounce red food coloring

2 1/2 cups cake flour

1/2 teaspoon salt

1 1/2 teaspoons baking soda

1 1/4 teaspoons baking powder

1 cup buttermilk

1 teaspoon vanilla extract

ICING:

1 cup milk

3 tablespoons flour

1 cup butter

1 cup sugar

1 teaspoon vanilla extract

1/2 cup chopped pecans (optional)

1 Preheat the oven to 350 degrees.

2 **To make the cake**, in a large bowl cream together the sugar, butter, and eggs. Add the vinegar, cocoa, and food coloring and mix well. Add the flour, salt, baking soda, baking powder, buttermilk, and vanilla and mix well. Pour the batter into a greased 13 x 9-inch baking pan.

3 Bake for 30 minutes, or until a toothpick inserted in the center comes out clean. Cool before frosting.

4 **TO MAKE THE ICING,** mix the milk and flour in a saucepan. Cook over medium-low heat until thick, approximately 10 minutes. Cover and refrigerate until completely chilled. In the bowl of an electric mixer, beat the butter, sugar, and vanilla on high until creamy. Add the chilled milk and flour mixture and beat until light and fluffy, 6 to 8 minutes. Ice the cooled cake and top with pecans, if desired. Refrigerate the cake before and after serving.

MAKES 10 TO 12 SERVINGS.

JESSICA SCHIMDONSKI (Mount Juliet, Tennessee) says that her Grandma Mamie, MAMIE OSBORNE (Blytheville, Arkansas), was the best cook she's ever known and this cake is sinfully delicious. Jessica also shares that Mamie was certainly a character. "While she's been gone since 1994, we never stop telling stories at family get-togethers," Jessica says. "Everything was always perfect. I would stay with her most every summer, and she taught me how to be a lady in the parlor and a mean poker player in the meantime. Mamie was always cooking for all of us—our favorite memories are based on her kitchen creations and the poker table."

CAKE:

2 sticks butter

2 cups sugar

4 large eggs

I teaspoon baking soda

½ cup buttermilk

3 ½ cups all-purpose flour

I pound chopped dates

I pound orange-slice candy, chopped

2 cups chopped pecans

I ⅓ cups sweetened shredded coconut

GLAZE:

I cup orange juice

2 cups powdered sugar

1 Preheat the oven to 350 degrees.

2 TO MAKE THE CAKE, cream the butter and sugar in a large bowl. Beat in the eggs, one at a time. Dissolve the baking soda in the buttermilk and then add to the bowl. Add the flour, dates, orange candy, pecans, and coconut and mix well. (The mixture will be very stiff.) Spoon the batter into a greased and floured Bundt pan.

3 Bake for I hour and 45 minutes, or until a toothpick inserted in the center comes out clean. Remove from pan onto serving plate. Frost immediately.

4 TO MAKE THE GLAZE, combine the orange juice and powdered sugar in a medium bowl. Pour the glaze over the hot cake and let the cake stand overnight before serving.

MAKES 10 TO 12 SERVINGS.

NANNY'S LADY BALTIMORE CAKE

KATHERINE FINCH (Forrest City, Arkansas) shares that her family cherishes this favorite holiday cake. Nanny's cakes were beyond fantastic—you hesitated to slice them because they were so elegant. While Nanny, **CLARA LILLIAN VERNON WADE** (Fort Smith, Arkansas), had a full-size kitchen downstairs, she preferred to do her baking upstairs because she liked that oven better. This cake was a special favorite of Kathy's grandfather—in fact, he'd even chop the ingredients if Nanny would make it for him. At Christmas, Nanny would place whole maraschino cherries on the top of the cake to make it festive.

CAKE:

2 sticks butter

2 cups sugar

3 1/2 cups all-purpose flour, sifted

3 teaspoons baking powder

1 cup milk

6 large egg whites

1 teaspoon vanilla or lemon extract

ICING:

2 large egg whites

2 1/4 cups sugar

1/2 cup light corn syrup

1/8 teaspoon salt

1/2 cup water

1 teaspoon vanilla extract

2/3 cup chopped raisins

2/3 cup chopped walnuts

12 maraschino cherries, drained and chopped

1 Preheat the oven to 375 degrees.

2 **TO MAKE THE CAKE**, cream the butter in a large bowl and beat in the sugar. Combine the flour and baking powder in a medium bowl. Add the flour mixture alternately with the milk, mixing well after each addition. In a separate medium bowl beat the egg whites until stiff and then fold them into the cake mixture. Add the vanilla or lemon extract and stir. Pour the batter into 2 lightly greased and floured 12 x 9-inch baking pans.

3 Bake for 25 minutes, or until a toothpick in the center comes out clean. Allow cake to cool completely before frosting.

4 **To make the icing**, stiffly beat the egg whites in a medium bowl. In a saucepan cook the sugar, corn syrup, salt, and water until the mixture reaches 246 degrees, as measured with a candy thermometer. Slowly beat the hot syrup into the stiffly beaten egg whites. Mix in the vanilla. Set aside 1 cup of the icing for the top of the cake. To make the filling, add the raisins, walnuts, and cherries to the remaining icing and beat in briskly. Spread the fruit and nut filling between the cake layers (about 1-inch thick). Cover the top and sides of the cake with a thin layer of the plain icing.

MAKES 8 SERVINGS.

MAMAW'S STRAWBERRY PUDDING CAKE

ALISON HARRIS (Murfreesboro, Tennessee) says, "Every time we go to visit my Mamaw, she always has a ton of food made for us!" Mamaw is **NAOMA MAINES** (Morehead, Kentucky). "She loves to cook and bake and when we spend the night, she always has a huge breakfast prepared each morning for us," Alison says. "She's a wonderful lady I admire so much!"

1 box (18.25 ounces)
  yellow cake mix

3 large eggs

1/2 cup vegetable oil

1/2 cup water

1 box (1.5 ounces)
  instant vanilla or
  lemon pudding

2 cups milk

2 cups mashed
  strawberries

1/4 cup sugar

1 container (8
  ounces) frozen
  whipped topping,
  thawed

12 maraschino
  cherries, halved

1 Preheat the oven to 350 degrees.

2 Add the cake mix, eggs, oil, and water to a large bowl and mix well. Pour the batter into a greased and floured 13 x 9-inch glass baking pan.

3 In a small bowl combine the pudding mix with the milk and beat until all lumps are gone. Pour the prepared pudding over the top of the cake batter.

4 In a separate small bowl mix the mashed strawberries with the sugar. Spoon the strawberry mixture on top of the pudding mixture.

5 Bake for 35 to 40 minutes, or until the cake is firm and a toothpick inserted in the center comes out clean. Cool the cake completely. Before serving, spread the whipped topping on top of the cake and decorate with the maraschino cherries. Refrigerate any leftover cake.

MAKES 10 TO 12 SERVINGS.

LIZZIE'S SOUR CREAM POUND CAKE

ARLENE RAINES (Goodlettsville, Tennessee) shares that her grandma, **MARY ELIZABETH REDDING HUGHES**, was affectionately known as Lizzie. "Lizzie and her husband owned and worked a 300-acre farm in Naylor, Georgia," Arlene says. "She was the quintessential countrywoman who raised her children, worked the fields, cooked for the farmhands, sewed her children's clothing, and kept the house. My grandmother was a wonderful cook and one of my favorite things was this pound cake. The entire farmhouse would smell wonderful while it was baking, and the cake only became more delicious each day that it sat under a glass cover on the kitchen table. Grandma Lizzie died in 1986 at the age of ninety-seven, but she is remembered in a special way each year at our family reunion because her pound cake is always on the menu."

---

2 sticks butter, softened

3 cups sugar

6 large eggs, at room temperature

3 cups all-purpose flour

1/2 teaspoon baking powder

1/4 teaspoon baking soda

1 container (8 ounces) sour cream

1/2 teaspoon vanilla extract

1/2 teaspoon lemon extract

---

1 Preheat the oven to 325 degrees.

2 In the large bowl of an electric mixer, beat together the butter and sugar. Add 1 egg at a time, beating thoroughly after each addition. In a medium bowl sift together the flour, baking powder, and baking soda. Add the flour mixture to the batter and beat thoroughly. Add the sour cream, vanilla, and lemon extract and beat thoroughly. The secret is to beat lots and lots of air into the batter. Pour the batter into a greased and floured 10-inch tube pan.

3 Bake for 1 1/2 hours, or until a toothpick inserted in the center comes out clean. Cool before slicing.

MAKES 8 TO 10 SERVINGS.

MEMA'S PECAN BUNDT CAKE

EMMIE PACK (Nashville, Tennessee) is fortunate to have a great grandma. She calls her Mema. Emmie likes to visit Mema, **BERTHA DILLON** (Crossville, Tennessee), because she always has homemade sweet treats for Emmie and her sister, Massey. Mema also makes really good cake and this is one of their mom's favorites.

1 cup pecans

2 tablespoons ground cinnamon

2 tablespoons firmly packed brown sugar

1 package (18.25 ounces) butter cake mix

3/4 cup vegetable oil

1/2 cup sugar

1 teaspoon butter flavoring

1 container (8 ounces) sour cream

4 large eggs

1 Preheat the oven to 350 degrees.

2 In a small bowl mix the pecans, cinnamon, and brown sugar and set aside.

3 In a large bowl mix the cake mix, oil, sugar, butter flavoring, sour cream, and eggs.

4 Pour half of the batter into a greased and floured Bundt pan. Sprinkle all of the pecan mixture over the batter. Pour the other half of the batter over the pecan mixture.

5 Bake for 50 to 60 minutes, or until a toothpick inserted in the center comes out clean. Cool the cake for about 30 minutes before removing from the pan.

MAKES 10 TO 12 SERVINGS.

MOM'S GINGERBREAD

SUSAN GENTRY WILLIAMS (Nashville, Tennessee) called her grandmother Mom. FLORA LETT BRYANT (Johnson City, Tennessee) had no cookbooks, just a few cards with favorite recipes she had written down to share with her garden club. This recipe was among them. Susan says, "My cousin Nancy and I often spent the night with Mom, staying in what had been a large dormer closet, but was then turned into a little bunk cubby for children. We giggled into the night and when we awakened in the morning, it was to smells of coffee and gingerbread, hot from her oven."

CAKE:

2 ½ cups all-purpose flour

1 ½ teaspoons baking soda

1 teaspoon ground cinnamon

1 teaspoon ground ginger

½ teaspoon ground cloves

½ teaspoon salt

¼ cup firmly packed brown sugar

¼ cup white sugar

1 stick butter

1 large egg

1 cup dark molasses

1 cup hot water

SAUCE:

½ cup sugar

1 tablespoon cornstarch

1 cup boiling water

pinch of salt

2 tablespoons lemon juice

2 tablespoons butter

pinch of ground nutmeg

1 Preheat the oven to 350 degrees.

2 TO MAKE THE CAKE, in a medium bowl sift together the flour, baking soda, cinnamon, ginger, cloves, and salt. In a large bowl cream together the brown sugar, white sugar, and butter. Add the egg and molasses and blend together. Add the flour mixture and the hot water to the butter mixture and mix well. Pour the batter into a greased 9-inch square baking pan.

3 Bake for 60 minutes, or until a toothpick inserted in the center comes out clean. Add the sauce while still warm.

4 To **MAKE THE SAUCE**, mix the sugar and cornstarch in the top of a double boiler on medium-high heat. Add the boiling water and salt and cook until the mixture is clear. Cook for another 20 minutes over medium heat, stirring constantly. Remove from the heat and beat the lemon juice, butter, and nutmeg into the mixture and pour over the warm gingerbread. Serve warm.

MAKES 8 TO 10 SERVINGS.

ESTHER'S PUMPKIN CAKE

KALEE GREGG (Richmond, Kentucky) is one of five granddaughters that Grammy **ESTHER ELAINE FERKAN GREGG** (Lexington, Kentucky) had. Kalee and her two sisters were spoiled by Grammy from the time they were born. "I remember her sewing princess dresses for my older sister and me. We later wore the dresses at a tea party she attended with us," Kalee says. "We really miss her." She passed away in 2008.

---

2 cups all-purpose flour

2 teaspoons baking powder

2 teaspoons ground cinnamon

1 teaspoon baking soda

1/4 teaspoon salt

4 large eggs

1 can (15 ounces) pumpkin

1 2/3 cups sugar

1 cup vegetable oil

1/4 cup chopped pecans or walnuts (optional)

---

1 Preheat the oven to 350 degrees.
2 Combine the flour, baking powder, cinnamon, baking soda, and salt in a medium bowl and set aside. In a large bowl beat the eggs, pumpkin, sugar, and oil. Add the flour mixture to the pumpkin mixture and beat until well combined. If desired, add the nuts and mix well. Pour into an ungreased 13 x 9-inch baking pan.
3 Bake for 25 to 30 minutes, or until a toothpick inserted in the center comes out clean. Cool on a wire rack. When cool, spread with your favorite cream cheese icing or sprinkle with powdered sugar, if desired.

MAKES 10 TO 12 SERVINGS.

✤✤✤ COCA-COLA CAKE

KIM HOFFMAN (Hendersonville, Tennessee) shares her favorite recipe from Grandma **BUNA JORDAN** (Montgomery, Alabama). "Grandma always fixed this, my favorite cake, when my family came to visit," Kim says. "And she usually ended up making two cakes—one with nuts for me and one without nuts for my brother!"

CAKE:

2 cups all-purpose flour

2 cups sugar

1 ½ cups small marshmallows

1 stick butter

½ cup vegetable oil

3 tablespoons cocoa

1 cup Coca-Cola

1 teaspoon baking soda

½ cup buttermilk

2 large eggs

1 teaspoon vanilla extract

ICING:

1 package (16 ounces) powdered sugar

1 stick butter

3 tablespoons cocoa

6 tablespoons Coca-Cola

1 teaspoon vanilla extract

1 cup chopped pecans

1 Preheat the oven to 350 degrees.

2 **TO MAKE THE CAKE**, sift together the flour and sugar in a large bowl. Add the marshmallows.

3 In a medium saucepan mix the butter, oil, cocoa, and Coca-Cola. Bring to a boil and pour over the flour mixture. Mix well.

4 In a small bowl dissolve the baking soda in the buttermilk. Pour the buttermilk mixture into the batter. Add the eggs and vanilla and mix well. Pour the batter into a well-greased 13 x 9-inch baking pan.

5 Bake for 35 to 45 minutes, or until a toothpick inserted in the center comes out clean. Frost immediately.

6 **TO MAKE THE ICING**, put the powdered sugar in a medium bowl and set aside. In a medium saucepan combine the butter, cocoa, and Coca-Cola. Bring to a boil and pour over the powdered sugar, blending well. Add the vanilla and pecans and mix well. Spread over the hot cake. When the cake is cool, cut it into squares and serve.

MAKES 10 TO 12 SERVINGS.

ESTHER'S APPLE CAKE

TAYLOR GREGG (Richmond, Kentucky) is third in the line of five granddaughters that Grammy **ESTHER ELAINE FERKAN GREGG** (Lexington, Kentucky) had. Taylor and her two sisters loved to be spoiled by Grammy and spend the night at her house. Taylor says, "She was a great cook and baker and I remember her putting vanilla ice cream and milk in a glass and stirring it up to make milk shakes for me and my two sisters. She also sewed things for us. I really miss her." She passed away in 2008.

CAKE:
2 sticks butter

3/4 cup white sugar

1 large egg

1 cup milk

2 teaspoons vanilla extract

3 cups all-purpose flour

1/2 teaspoon baking powder

2 teaspoons baking soda

1 teaspoon salt

1/4 teaspoon ground cinnamon

4 cups peeled and chopped apples

TOPPING:
1 cup firmly packed brown sugar

4 teaspoons all-purpose flour

4 teaspoons ground cinnamon

1/2 stick butter

3/4 cup chopped walnuts

1 Preheat the oven to 350 degrees.

2 **TO MAKE THE CAKE**, blend the butter, white sugar, and egg in a large bowl. Add the milk, vanilla, flour, baking powder, baking soda, salt, and cinnamon and mix well. Add the apples and mix well. Pour the batter into a greased 13 x 9-inch baking pan.

3 **TO MAKE THE TOPPING**, blend the brown sugar, flour, cinnamon, butter, and walnuts in a small bowl and sprinkle on top of the batter.

4 Bake for 45 minutes, or until a toothpick inserted in the center comes out clean. Cool for 60 minutes before cutting.

MAKES 10 TO 12 SERVINGS.

Cookies

Peanut Butter Blossoms

Arkansas Traveler Cookies

Chocolate Fork Cookies

Grandmother Jacks's Tea Cakes

Lemon Tea Cakes

Tiny Tea Cakes

Mema's Chocolate-Chip Cookies

Peanut Butter Cookies

Feel-Better Cookies

Crescent Cookies

MawMaw's Oatmeal Cookies

Cowboy Cookies

PEANUT BUTTER BLOSSOMS

Gran is what **LIBBY ELLIOTT** (Burns, Tennessee) calls her grandma, **BETTY JO ELLIOTT** (Charlotte, Tennessee). Libby says, "Every time I'd go to Gran's house, we would bake cookies. The dough was, and still is, my favorite. These particular cookies are the ones I always leave for Santa Claus." Libby also shares that when she'd spend the night at Gran's, Gran would quite often read her the book *The Best-Loved Doll*.

3 cups all-purpose flour

2 teaspoons baking soda

2 teaspoons salt

2 sticks butter

1 cup peanut butter (smooth or crunchy)

1 package (16 ounces) brown sugar

2 large eggs

2 tablespoons vanilla extract

1/4 cup sugar

36 Hershey's Kisses, unwrapped

1 Preheat the oven to 350 degrees.

2 In a medium bowl sift together the flour, baking soda, and salt. In a large bowl cream together the butter, peanut butter, brown sugar, eggs, and vanilla. Add the flour mixture to the creamed mixture and mix well.

3 Using your hands, shape the batter into 1-inch balls and roll in the sugar. Place the sugared balls on ungreased cookie sheets about 2 inches apart.

4 Bake for 7 minutes. Take the pan out of the oven and immediately place a chocolate kiss in the center of each cookie and press down. Put the cookies back in the oven and bake for just 1 additional minute. Remove from the oven and allow to cool before eating.

MAKES 3 DOZEN COOKIES.

ARKANSAS TRAVELER COOKIES

MARY MITCHELL (Nashville, Tennessee) says that her grandmother, **MABLE MASON TODD** (McMinnville, Tennessee), raised her and her brother after their mother died. Mable was born in Texas but was then raised in the hills of Cannon County, Tennessee. "Grandmother always told me, 'Pretty is as pretty does and you have to act pretty to be pretty,'" Mary says. "I really didn't appreciate her as I should have until I aged and wondered how in the world she raised two little children in her late fifties—the age I am now. She was the cook at Bethany, a small country school. She was very thrifty and didn't believe in waste. 'Waste not, want not' was one of her sayings too. I learned so much from her and feel I am a lot like her."

2 sticks butter	2 large eggs	3 cups all-purpose flour, sifted
1 cup white sugar	1 teaspoon vanilla extract	2 teaspoons baking powder
1 cup firmly packed brown sugar	1 cup peanut butter	

1 Preheat the oven to 350 degrees.
2 In a large bowl cream together the butter, white sugar, and brown sugar. Add the eggs and vanilla and mix well. Blend in the peanut butter. Mix in the flour and baking powder.
3 Roll the dough into balls the size of a small walnut. Place the balls on ungreased cookie sheets and mash slightly with a fork.
4 Bake for 8 to 10 minutes, making sure bottoms don't get too brown. Do not overbake. Cool for 2 minutes on the cookie sheet before transferring to a wire rack to cool.

MAKES 3 TO 4 DOZEN COOKIES.

CHOCOLATE FORK COOKIES

"These cookies are best enjoyed with a really tall glass of milk," says **CHRISTIN BROWN** (Nunnelly, Tennessee). When making these cookies, her Granny used to say, "Add some flour . . . some more . . . some more . . . stop!" Granny is **DEBBIE CASTILLO**—she was born in Biloxi, Mississippi, and now lives in Bon Aqua, Tennessee. Christin says that she and her twin sister used to like eating some of Granny's biscuit dough. They also got a kick out of many of Granny's sayings.

I cup sugar

I tablespoon cocoa

I large egg

3 tablespoons vegetable oil

2 cups self-rising flour

---

1 Preheat the oven to 350 degrees.

2 Combine the sugar and cocoa in a large bowl. Stir in the egg and oil. Gradually add the flour. You will need to add more flour if the dough is too sticky to roll into balls by hand.

3 Using your hands, roll the dough into small balls (about the size of a Ping-Pong ball) and place on greased cookie sheets about I inch apart. Before baking, dip a fork into a small cup of water. Gently mash the fork into the tops of the cookies.

4 Bake for just 6 to 7 minutes, removing when the cookies are still a little doughy in the center. Be careful not to overbake or they will be rock hard. Cool on a wire rack.

MAKES 2 DOZEN COOKIES.

GRANDMOTHER JACKS'S TEA CAKES

GINNY STAGGS (Nashville, Tennessee) says that Grandmother **ZELL HARDIN JACKS** was born around 1900 and raised three sons with Grandfather Raymon in Lincoln County, Tennessee. A proud woman, she taught her grandchildren to call her Grandmother, never Granny or Grandma. She utilized what was available from the garden or the freezer, always using the simplest ingredients and rarely referring to a recipe. Ginny says, "This recipe was shared with me verbally, which is likely the first time it was ever written down— it's a perfect example of simple comfort from Grandmother's kitchen."

COOKIES:

1/2 cup margarine, softened

1 cup sugar

1/2 teaspoon ground nutmeg

2 large eggs

2 cups self-rising flour

TOPPING:

2 tablespoons sugar

1/4 teaspoon ground nutmeg

1 Preheat the oven to 375 degrees.

2 **TO MAKE THE COOKIES**, cream the margarine and sugar in a large bowl. Add the nutmeg and mix well. Add the eggs and flour and mix well. Knead by hand until stiff. Add more flour if needed to make a stiff dough.

3 Roll out the dough to a 1/4-inch thickness and cut with a 2 1/2-inch cookie cutter. Place on greased cookie sheets.

4 Bake for about 10 minutes, or until the cookies begin to brown. Transfer to a wire rack to cool.

5 **TO MAKE THE TOPPING**, mix the sugar and nutmeg in small bowl. Sprinkle the cooled cookies with the nutmeg and sugar mixture.

MAKES 18 TO 24 TEA CAKES.

❖❖❖ LEMON TEA CAKES

KATHARINE RAY (Nashville, Tennessee) says that her Granny, TOMMIE GLASSCOCK (Shelbyville, Tennessee), was the master of the quintessential Southern noontime "dinner." Katharine says, "With great ease, working in an apron and a simple cotton housedress she made herself, she turned out a daily small feast for whoever might be stopping by, including any family member or friend down on his luck who knew that Mama/Tomcat/Aunt Tommy would be ready with the likes of ham or roast beef, green beans, macaroni and cheese, fresh fried corn, sliced home-grown tomatoes, lime Jell-O salad, cornbread and biscuits made each day from scratch, and fresh coconut cake. Her skill looked effortless to me. Following the midday meal, Granny moved what was left of the feast to the table in the kitchen and covered it with a checkered tablecloth. I learned to peek under that cloth to scan the leftovers there for the taking. The best prize, undoubtedly, was her from-scratch tea cakes with a hint of lemon. My older sister and I would grab fistfuls and scurry outside. Made with the simplest ingredients, they were perfection. Today, when I hear the words 'tea cake,' I'm taken right back to the magic I would find under that tablecloth and Granny's nurturing love for her family."

---

2 sticks butter, softened

1 1/4 cups sugar

1 teaspoon lemon extract

2 large eggs

1 teaspoon lemon zest

3 cups all-purpose flour

1 teaspoon baking soda

1/4 teaspoon salt

3 tablespoons buttermilk

sugar for sprinkling

---

1 Preheat the oven to 350 degrees.

2 In the bowl of an electric mixer, beat the butter on medium speed for 1 minute, until light. Add the sugar and the lemon extract and beat until light and fluffy. Add the eggs and lemon zest and beat well. Mix the flour, baking soda, and salt in a medium bowl. Add the flour mixture and the buttermilk alternately to the butter mixture, beating well after each addition.

3 Drop the cookies by rounded teaspoonfuls onto greased cookie sheets. Sprinkle with white sugar.

4 Bake for 10 to 12 minutes, or until lightly browned on the edges. Transfer to a wire rack to cool.

MAKES 4 DOZEN COOKIES.

Mama, **MYRTLE KELLY**, made the best tea cakes, according to granddaughter **NELL KELLY** (Alexander City, Alabama). Her recipe dates back to 1936—and this version is unique because the "cakes" are tiny and deliciously light and crisp. Southern-raised girls share sweet memories of their grandmothers making these cookies. Since a lot of recipes weren't written down back then, many learned to make tea cakes by watching and listening to their grandmothers. Most tea cakes contain the basic ingredients—sugar, flour, vanilla, eggs—but along the way, some cooks have developed their own varieties by adding things like nuts, lemon or orange rind, molasses, cinnamon, and other spices or flavorings. Recipes vary, so some tea cakes resemble shortbread, some are soft with a cake-like texture, and others are thin and crisp like sugar cookies.

---

2 sticks butter

1/2 cup firmly packed light brown sugar

1/2 cup white sugar

I large egg, beaten

2 cups all-purpose flour

1/8 teaspoon salt

I teaspoon vanilla extract

Decorative cherries or nuts (optional)

---

1 Preheat the oven to 375 degrees.

2 In a large bowl cream together the butter, brown sugar, and white sugar. Add the egg and mix well. Blend in the flour and salt. Add the vanilla and mix well.

3 Drop by rounded 1/2 teaspoonfuls onto greased cookie sheets.

4 Bake for 7 to 9 minutes, or until lightly browned. If desired, decorate each with a cherry or nut before baking.

MAKES 30 TO 36 COOKIES.

MEMA'S CHOCOLATE-CHIP COOKIES

Anytime **ANN PACK** (Nashville, Tennessee) visited her Mema, **BERTHA DILLON** (Crossville, Tennessee), she was always included in the cooking and baking process. "Our favorite thing to make together was chocolate-chip cookies," Ann recalls. "Mema always brought a stool or a kitchen chair for me to stand on so that I could reach the counter. We always wore our little aprons and we had so much fun."

2 1/4 cups all-purpose flour

1/4 teaspoon salt

I teaspoon baking soda

3/4 cup white sugar

I cup firmly packed brown sugar

I stick butter, softened

2 teaspoons vanilla extract

2 large egg whites

3/4 cup semisweet chocolate chips

cooking spray

1 Preheat the oven to 350 degrees.

2 In a medium bowl combine the flour, salt, and baking soda, stirring with a whisk to remove any clumps. In the bowl of an electric mixer, beat the white sugar, brown sugar, and butter at medium speed until well blended. Add the vanilla and egg whites and beat for 1 1/2 minutes. Add the flour mixture and the chocolate chips and beat until blended.

3 Spray cookie sheets with cooking spray. Drop the dough by level tablespoonfuls onto the cookie sheets, placing the cookies about 2 inches apart.

4 Bake for 10 minutes, or until lightly browned. Cool the cookies on the cookie sheets for 3 minutes and then transfer to wire racks to cool.

MAKES 3 DOZEN COOKIES.

PEANUT BUTTER COOKIES

Ma is what **KAREN BASKIN** (Mount Juliet, Tennessee) called her grandma. Ma, **MARTHA NANNIE STAFFORD** (Gainesboro, Tennessee), used to say, "You might as well laugh as to cry," and that's how she lived her life. "She had such a positive attitude and was always smiling and laughing, no matter the hardships she was facing," Karen recalls. "Ma also loved Halloween—for years she made homemade popcorn balls to give out as treats. She also loved to dress up and play practical jokes on people. One time, she disguised herself as a hobo and even fooled my grandfather—he had no idea it was her."

½ cup shortening

½ cup peanut butter

½ cup firmly packed brown sugar

½ cup white sugar

1 large egg

½ teaspoon vanilla extract

1 ½ cups self-rising flour

1 Preheat the oven to 350 degrees.

2 In a large bowl cream together the shortening, peanut butter, brown sugar, white sugar, egg, and vanilla. Gradually add the flour and mix well.

3 Form the dough into 1-inch balls and place on greased cookie sheets. Flatten with a fork to make crisscross marks.

4 Bake for 12 to 15 minutes, or until lightly browned on the bottoms. Cool on a wire rack.

MAKES 18 TO 24 COOKIES.

FEEL-BETTER COOKIES

Amy Gregg (Lexington, Kentucky) says her grandma, **Euldean Bessie Bow**, lived in Bow, Kentucky. Grandma Bow loved to make and share these comfort treats. She claimed that these chocolate marshmallow cookies were the best in the world, "guaranteed to make any girl feel better when life is more challenging than expected." So listen to Grandma B. and make you up a batch to share!

COOKIES:

1 3/4 cups all-purpose flour, sifted

1/2 teaspoon baking soda

1/2 teaspoon salt

1/2 cup cocoa

1/2 cup shortening

1 cup sugar

1 large egg

1/2 cup milk

1 teaspoon vanilla extract

36 marshmallows, cut in half

ICING:

2 tablespoons butter

5 tablespoons cocoa

4 teaspoons milk

2 1/2 cups powdered sugar

---

1. Preheat the oven to 350 degrees.
2. **To make the cookies**, mix the flour, baking soda, salt, and cocoa in a medium bowl. In the bowl of an electric mixer, beat the shortening, sugar, egg, milk, and vanilla until fluffy. Gradually add the flour mixture and stir with a wooden spoon until thoroughly mixed.
3. On a lightly floured work surface, roll out the dough to a 1/4-inch thickness. Cut out the cookies with a circular cookie cutter and place the cookies 2 inches apart on ungreased cookie sheets.
4. Bake for 8 minutes, remove from the oven, and place a halved marshmallow (cut side down) on each cookie. Return the cookie sheet to the oven and bake for 2 more minutes to melt the marshmallows. Allow the cookies to cool on the cookie sheets for 5 minutes before transferring to a wire rack to finish cooling.

5 **TO MAKE THE ICING**, combine the butter, cocoa, and milk in a medium bowl and stir until well blended. Gradually add the powdered sugar and beat until well blended. Spread the icing on the cookies when cool.

MAKES 3 DOZEN COOKIES.

CRESCENT COOKIES

Great food fills **PAIGE ANDERSON'S** (Nashville, Tennessee) memories of childhood with her Memi Jackie, **JACQUELYN B. ANDERSON** (also of Nashville). From a meal as lavish as a Christmas dinner to one as simple as a Sunday breakfast, good food had a starring role in her home and on her table. And despite all the hours of work, preparation, and love that Memi puts into her dishes, she makes each creation seem effortless—incredible meals flow from her hands as easily and warmly as hugs from her arms and love from her heart. These cookies are a favorite holiday treat for Paige.

2 sticks butter, softened

2 cups all-purpose flour

1 cup finely chopped pecans

1 teaspoon vanilla extract

powdered sugar for dusting

1 Preheat the oven to 325 degrees.

2 In a large bowl combine the butter, flour, pecans, and vanilla extract until the mixture forms a dough.

3 Form the dough into 1-inch balls. Roll out each ball slightly and curve it to create a crescent shape. Place the cookies 1 inch apart on ungreased cookie sheets.

4 Bake for 15 minutes, until lightly browned on the bottom. Cool completely and then dust the cookies with powdered sugar.

MAKES 20 TO 25 COOKIES.

MAWMAW'S OATMEAL COOKIES

KRISTEN ORR (Nashville, Tennessee) says that her MawMaw, **CATHERINE ORR** (Ashland City, Tennessee), made the most amazing desserts for every family occasion— usually cookies, cakes, pies, and fried pies. Kristen says, "MawMaw was born and raised in Henry County, Tennessee, and was known to always say, 'Oh, goodness gracious!' She likely said that and a few other choice words after I talked her into seeing *Return of the Jedi* when I was a teenager—I got her to go by telling her it was a love story."

1 stick margarine	1 teaspoon vanilla extract	2 tablespoons cocoa
2 cups sugar	½ cup milk	2 ½ cups rolled oats

1 In a large saucepan combine the margarine, sugar, vanilla, milk, and cocoa. Mix well and boil, stirring occasionally, for no more than 3 minutes. Remove from the heat, add the oats, and mix well.

2 Drop by rounded teaspoonfuls onto wax paper. Once cooled and hardened, they are ready to eat.

MAKES 2 DOZEN COOKIES.

COWBOY COOKIES ❈ ❈

AMY MAJORS (Fort Worth, Texas) says her grandma, **EVELYN BROWN** (also of Fort Worth), was a loud and proud Texas lady. "She was very proud of her heritage and loved to make things that had names attributed to her home state," Amy recalls. "Having grown up on a ranch, Grandma knew all about cowboys. One of my earliest memories of baking with her were these cowboy cookies. I make them with my children now."

3 sticks butter

1 1/2 cups white sugar

1 1/2 cups brown sugar

3 large eggs

1 tablespoon vanilla extract

3 cups all-purpose flour

1 tablespoon baking powder

1 teaspoon salt

1 tablespoon ground cinnamon

3 cups rolled oats

2 cups sweetened coconut flakes

2 cups chopped pecans

3 cups chocolate chips

1 Preheat the oven to 350 degrees.

2 In a large bowl cream together the butter, white sugar, and brown sugar. Add the eggs and vanilla and mix well. Add the flour, baking powder, salt, and cinnamon and mix well. Blend in the oats, coconut, pecans, and chocolate chips.

3 Drop by rounded teaspoonfuls onto ungreased cookie sheets.

4 Bake for 10 minutes or until lightly browned. Don't overbake. Transfer to a wire rack to cool.

MAKES 5 TO 6 DOZEN COOKIES.

Chocolate Pies

Sarah's Chocolate Pie
Nanny's Chocolate Pie
The "Wright" Fudge Nut Pie
Chocolate Chess Pie
Grandmother Kelly's Chocolate Pie
Chocolate Meringue Pie
Black Bottom Pie

SARAH'S CHOCOLATE PIE

JANICE GLASSCOCK (Nashville, Tennessee) remembers her Granny, **SARAH VANCE WILLIAMS DEERING** (Shelbyville, Tennessee), saying, "Heaven will be a great meetin'!" Janice says, "Granny's early-morning breakfasts were the best. I'd wake up in her bed to the smell of bacon frying and biscuits baking, as her kitchen was just off the bedroom. She'd come in and stoke up the fireplace and I would lie under the covers shivering until the room warmed up, then I'd scramble into the oven-warmed kitchen to eat, sipping on coffee with lots of milk and sugar at eight years of age."

---

3 tablespoons cocoa

1 ½ cups sugar

½ cup all-purpose flour

⅛ teaspoon salt

1 ½ cups boiling water

½ stick butter

1 teaspoon vanilla extract

1 pie crust (9 inches), unbaked

Whipped cream (optional)

---

1 Preheat the oven to 350 degrees.

2 Combine the cocoa, sugar, flour, salt, and water in a medium saucepan. Cook over medium heat, stirring constantly, until thickened, 3 to 5 minutes. Continue cooking and add the butter and vanilla and stir well. Remove from the heat when the butter has melted. Pour the mixture into the pie crust.

3 Bake for 30 minutes, or until the mixture sets. Cool on a wire rack before serving. If desired, top pie with whipped cream before serving.

MAKES 6 TO 8 SERVINGS.

# NANNY'S CHOCOLATE PIE

Shannon Scully McRae (Dothan, Alabama) remembers that when visiting Nanny, **Frances Kell** (Chandler Mountain, Alabama), on the weekend, Nanny would wake up much earlier than everyone else on Sunday mornings. "By the time I opened my eyes, the house already smelled like pinto beans or fried okra or some other food that you didn't normally eat in the morning," Shannon says. "Before she left the house for church, Nanny would have an entire meal for twelve people ready to eat the moment everyone walked into her house after church. I didn't think much of it at the time, but now as an adult, I'm amazed at her ability to multitask! On Sundays, when my husband and I can barely get ourselves and our two young children dressed and in the car to be on time for church, I often smile and think of Nanny, wondering how in the world she was able to prepare such a feast on Sunday mornings."

CRUST:
I 1/2 cups all-purpose flour

1/2 teaspoon salt

1/2 cup shortening

4 to 5 tablespoons water

FILLING:
I 1/2 cups sugar

2 cups milk

4 tablespoons cornstarch

4 tablespoons cocoa

3 large egg yolks (reserve whites for meringue)

2 tablespoons butter

I teaspoon vanilla extract

MERINGUE:
3 egg whites

3 tablespoons sugar

1 Preheat the oven to 450 degrees.

2 **To make the crust,** in a medium bowl use a fork or pastry cutter to combine the flour, salt, and shortening until crumbly. Add the water, I tablespoon at a time, until the dough is moist but not wet. On a well-floured work surface, roll out the dough with a rolling pin. Place the dough in a 9-inch pie pan and bake for 10 minutes. Remove from the oven and cool.

3 Reduce the oven temperature to 350 degrees.

4 To **MAKE THE FILLING**, combine the sugar, milk, cornstarch, and cocoa in a medium saucepan over medium heat. Beat the egg yolks in a large bowl, reserving the whites. When the chocolate mixture is well heated, slowly add it to the egg yolks, stirring continuously. Be careful to add it very slowly. Once combined, return the mixture to the saucepan and cook, stirring constantly, until it becomes very thick. Remove from the heat and add the butter and vanilla. Pour the mixture into the baked pie crust.

5 To **MAKE THE MERINGUE**, in a medium bowl beat the eggs whites with an electric mixer until stiff. Gradually beat in the sugar until soft peaks form. Spoon the meringue onto the pie, spreading it to the edges to seal it to the crust.

6 Bake for 10 minutes, or until the meringue is lightly browned. Cool on a wire rack before slicing.

MAKES 6 TO 8 SERVINGS.

THE "WRIGHT" FUDGE NUT PIE

Granddaughter **COURTNEY HINTON** (Hermitage, Tennessee) loves her grandma's fudge pie and the play on words with grandma's last name: "Wright" fudge pie / "right" fudge pie—get it? Grandma is **MARTHA WRIGHT**, who is originally from Mount Juliet, Tennessee, and currently resides in nearby Donelson. She is the proud mother of six children and eight grandchildren. Courtney shares that Grandma always hums a little tune when she's cooking.

2 squares (1 ounce each) unsweetened baking chocolate

1 stick butter

1 cup sugar

1/4 cup all-purpose flour

2 large eggs, slightly beaten

1 teaspoon vanilla extract

1 cup chopped pecans

1 pie crust (9 inches), unbaked

1 Preheat the oven to 350 degrees.
2 Melt the chocolate and butter in a small saucepan. Do not boil. In a medium bowl combine the sugar, flour, and eggs. Add the chocolate mixture, stirring while pouring it in. Add the vanilla and pecans and mix thoroughly. Pour the mixture into the pie crust.
3 Bake for 25 to 30 minutes, or until the center is firm. Serve warm or cool.

MAKES 8 SERVINGS.

CHOCOLATE CHESS PIE

SARAH SMITH (Tupelo, Mississippi) shares that her Mammy, **SARAH LANGSTON** (Saltillo, Mississippi), would always make chicken on Sunday afternoons. "She fried it in lard because that's how everybody cooked back then," Sarah says. "We always worked hard physically on our land, so there was no fear of getting heavy from eating fatty foods. And, speaking of working on the land, outside one day when I was a kid, a bee flew up Mammy's dress and was stinging her legs. My grandfather came to the rescue to get rid of the bee and lifted her dress over her head, displaying all of her undergarments. She was very embarrassed, of course, but our grandfather and all of us kids got a huge laugh out of it."

---

1 stick butter

2 squares (1 ounce each) unsweetened baking chocolate

1 cup sugar

2 tablespoons all-purpose flour

1/8 teaspoon salt

1/4 cup milk

3 large eggs, lightly beaten

1 1/2 teaspoons vanilla extract

1 pie crust (9 inches), unbaked

---

1 Preheat the oven to 350 degrees.

2 In a saucepan over low heat, melt the butter and chocolate. Transfer the chocolate mixture to the bowl of an electric mixer. Add the sugar, flour, salt, milk, eggs, and vanilla and beat for 5 to 6 minutes. Pour the filling into the pie crust.

3 Bake for 35 to 45 minutes, or until set. Cool for at least 30 minutes before serving.

MAKES 6 TO 8 SERVINGS.

GRANDMOTHER KELLY'S CHOCOLATE PIE

Momma Kelly was a good-hearted Christian woman, shares **REBECCA BLEWSTER FREE** (Siloam Springs, Arkansas). Momma Kelly was **NANCY SHEPHERD KELLY** (Lewisville, Arkansas). She had nine children and was a great cook. She always remembered each grandchild's birthday and Christmas, even if the gift was usually a pair of socks.

PIE:

1 ½ cups sugar

½ cup cocoa

¼ cup all-purpose flour

⅛ teaspoon salt

1 large egg, beaten

4 large egg yolks (reserve whites for meringue)

½ cup cold water

4 squares (1 ounce each) unsweetened baking chocolate

1 stick butter

1 tablespoon vanilla extract

1 cup boiling water

2 pie crusts (9 inches each), baked

MERINGUE:

4 large egg whites

½ teaspoon cream of tartar

½ cup sugar

1 Preheat the oven to 350 degrees.

2 TO MAKE THE PIE, mix the sugar, cocoa, and flour in a saucepan. Add the salt and mix well. Add the beaten egg and the 4 egg yolks one at a time. Add the cold water and mix well. Add the chocolate squares, butter, vanilla, and boiling water. Cook slowly over medium heat until the mixture is thick. Pour half of the mixture into each of the pie crusts.

3 TO MAKE THE MERINGUE, in a medium bowl beat the egg whites and cream of tartar with an electric mixer until stiff peaks form. Gradually add the sugar and continue beating. Spoon the meringue onto both pies, spreading it to the edges to seal it to the crust.

4 Bake for 10 minutes, or until the meringue is lightly browned. Cool pies on a wire rack before slicing.

MAKES 2 PIES.

CHOCOLATE MERINGUE PIE

KAREN BASKIN (Mount Juliet, Tennessee) says that her Ma, MARTHA NANNIE STAFFORD, was born in Gainesboro, Tennessee, in 1910 and lived her whole life there. Ma was a great Southern cook. She didn't have a lot of recipes written down because she mostly did everything by memory and by taste. It gave Ma great pleasure to cook a big meal for her family and friends.

PIE:

1 cup milk

1 cup sugar

3 tablespoons all-purpose flour

4 teaspoons cocoa

2 large egg yolks, beaten (reserve whites for meringue)

1 tablespoon butter

1 tablespoon vanilla extract

1 pie crust (9 inches), baked

MERINGUE:

2 large egg whites

1/4 cup sugar

1 Preheat the oven to 350 degrees.

2 **TO MAKE THE PIE**, in a large saucepan heat the milk over low heat until milk is heated through, approximately 5 minutes. In a small bowl blend the sugar, flour, and cocoa. Add the beaten egg yolks and mix well. Spoon the egg mixture into the saucepan and combine with the heated milk. Cook over low heat, stirring frequently, until the mixture is thick. Remove from heat and add the butter and vanilla and mix well until the butter melts. Pour the mixture into the baked pie crust.

3 **TO MAKE THE MERINGUE**, in the bowl of an electric mixer, whip the egg whites on medium speed for about 1 minute. Then whip on high for about 3 minutes. Gradually add the sugar and beat until stiff and glossy. Spoon the meringue evenly over the hot filling, spreading it to the edges to seal it to the crust.

4 Bake for approximately 10 minutes, or until the meringue is lightly browned. Cool on a wire rack before slicing.

MAKES 6 TO 8 SERVINGS.

 **BLACK BOTTOM PIE**

Christmas Eve was always Granny's day, shares **STACEY SMITH SHEFFIELD** (Nashville, Tennessee). The family would gather at her house and Granny, **ELIZABETH "BETTY" PORTRUM ROBERTSON** (Rogersville, Tennessee), would always make spaghetti for dinner with a sauce from scratch that included sliced green olives. "While it wasn't anything fancy or particularly Christmassy, we all loved it," Stacey says. "We'd then give her our Christmas gifts to open before we all went to church for communion. In 2004, Granny died three days before Christmas after a long, debilitating decline. To honor her memory, I made Granny's spaghetti for the entire family for Christmas Eve that year. It created a lot of conversation and warm reminiscences of Christmases past."

---

36 gingersnap cookies

1 stick butter, softened

1 cup sugar

2 teaspoons cornstarch

Pinch of salt

4 large eggs, separated

2 cups milk

1 teaspoon vanilla extract

2 squares (1 ounce each) unsweetened baking chocolate

1 envelope (1 tablespoon) unflavored gelatin

1/4 cup cold water

3 tablespoons rum

1/4 teaspoon cream of tartar

1 cup heavy cream

---

1 Preheat the oven to 300 degrees.

2 Place gingersnap cookies in a Ziploc bag and use a mallet or hammer to crush. In a large bowl mix the crushed cookies with the softened butter. Press the mixture into a greased 9-inch pie pan and bake for 10 minutes. Let cool completely.

3 In a small bowl mix the sugar, cornstarch, salt, and egg yolks. Bring the milk to a simmer in the top of a double boiler. Slowly add 1/2 cup of the hot milk to the yolk mixture, stirring constantly. Add the yolk mixture and the vanilla to the hot milk in the double boiler and mix well. Cook over low heat until the mixture is thick and coats a metal spoon. Remove from the heat. Transfer 1 1/4 cups of the hot mixture to a small bowl and add the chocolate. Stir until the chocolate is melted and allow to cool. Pour the chocolate mixture into the cooled pie crust and place in the refrigerator.

4 Combine the gelatin with the cold water in a small bowl and set aside to soften (5 minutes). Add the gelatin mixture to the remaining yolk mixture, stir well, and allow to cool. Stir the rum into the mixture.

5 In a medium bowl combine the egg whites and cream of tartar. Beat until stiff peaks form. Fold in the gelatin mixture. Spoon over the chocolate layer in the pie crust.

6 Whip the cream in a medium bowl until soft peaks form. Spread over the top of the pie. Chill in the refrigerator at least 2 hours before serving.

MAKES 6 TO 8 SERVINGS.

Bedtime-Snack Brownies (page 266)

Miscellaneous Desserts

Mamaw's Banana Pudding

Peanut Butter Buckeye Balls

Apple Crisp

Peach Ice Cream

Snow Cream

Mia's Boiled Custard

Pecan Pralines

Pumpkin Roll

Bug's Toffee

Chocolate Date-Nut Bars

Bedtime-Snack Brownies

K. K.'s Four-Chip Fudge

MAMAW'S BANANA PUDDING

JEANNIE HIGGINS (Greeneville, Tennessee) shares that this pudding is the one thing she's continued to make over and over again through the years, just as Mamaw taught her. Mamaw, **MARGARET HIPPS RICKER**, was born November 17, 1919, in Madison County, North Carolina, but lived most of her life in Greeneville, Tennessee.

2 large eggs, beaten

1/2 cup sugar

1/8 teaspoon salt

I teaspoon vanilla extract

4 tablespoons all-purpose flour

2 cups milk

3 medium-size ripe bananas, sliced

20 whole vanilla wafers* plus additional for crumbling

1 In the top of a double boiler, mix the eggs, sugar, salt, vanilla, and flour and cook over medium heat. Gradually add the milk and stir constantly as the pudding mixture thickens. Remove from the heat and allow the pudding to cool.

2 In a medium bowl layer the bananas, vanilla wafers (as many as needed), and pudding mixture. Crumble additional vanilla wafers (use the broken ones and the crumbs at the bottom of the box) on top and insert whole wafers around the edge of the pudding. Chill for 2 hours before serving.

MAKES 10 SERVINGS.

* You may need more, depending on the size of your bowl.

PEANUT BUTTER BUCKEYE BALLS

FAITH AND SARAH JONES (Thompson's Station, Tennessee) say that MawMaw's house would be the place to be in the event of a nuclear holocaust. MawMaw, **BEVERLY DAVIS** (Brentwood, Tennessee), has a huge pantry packed to the ceiling with more sugar-free Jell-O, cereal, Cheez-Its, macaroni and cheese, and so on than an army could eat. She still shops like she is feeding a family of twenty instead of just herself and Paw. Paw asked for some salad dressing the other day and she brought him twelve different varieties.

2 sticks butter

1 jar (18 ounces) chunky peanut butter

5 3/4 cups powdered sugar, sifted

cooking spray

1 bag (12 ounces) semisweet chocolate chips

1 tablespoon shortening

1 Melt the butter in a large microwave-safe bowl in the microwave. Add the peanut butter and mix until the peanut butter melts. Stir in the powdered sugar.

2 Using your hands, roll the mixture into 1-inch balls. Put a toothpick in each one and place on wax paper–covered cookie sheets sprayed with cooking spray. Place the cookie sheets in the freezer so the balls will harden, approximately 20 minutes.

3 Meanwhile, melt the chocolate chips and shortening in a double boiler. When the mixture is melted, remove the peanut butter balls from the freezer. Dip each ball in the chocolate, but leave a circle of peanut butter exposed on the top. Place the dipped balls back on the cookie sheets and place in the refrigerator for 30 minutes to harden.

MAKES 50 BALLS.

APPLE CRISP

Debby White (White House, Tennessee) shares that her Grandmother Frankie, **Frances Lane** (also of White House), raised five girls and one boy. "Frankie taught my mom and all of my aunts to cook," Debby says. "I remember the women all gathered around the table working as a team to cook whatever they felt a hankering for that day or whatever was in season. My cousin and I stayed outside but were the 'official' tasters. Even though we were skinny little girls, when the food was ready we ate like young pups until our tummies ached—it was such good food, it was worth it!"

4 large apples, peeled, cored, and sliced*

1/2 cup white sugar

3/4 cup firmly packed brown sugar

1/2 cup all-purpose flour

1/2 cup rolled oats

3/4 teaspoon ground cinnamon

3/4 teaspoon ground nutmeg

1/3 cup butter, softened

1 Preheat the oven to 350 degrees.

2 Place the apples in a greased 8-inch square baking pan and sprinkle them with the white sugar.

3 In a medium bowl blend the brown sugar, flour, oats, cinnamon, nutmeg, and butter until crumbly. Spread the mixture over the apples.

4 Bake for 35 minutes or until lightly browned. Serve warm plain or with whipped cream or vanilla ice cream.

MAKES 6 TO 8 SERVINGS.

* Granny Smith or Jonathan apples hold up well for baking.

PEACH ICE CREAM

MANDY HELTSLEY BUTTERS (Brentwood, Tennessee) shares that MaMaw, **HELEN SPARKS NICHOLS** (Greenville, Kentucky), would host big family dinners at her house with people crammed around the table, "using every odd chair we could find to fit everyone around the table. She'd say over and over, 'You haven't eaten a thing—you need to eat more!' Yet, we'd all eaten so much, we'd have to lie down after those big dinners and take a rest."

---

3 cups heavy whipping cream, divided

2 cups sugar, divided

2 large eggs

18 medium peaches, very ripe

---

1 In a medium bowl whip I cup of the heavy whipping cream. In a large bowl cream together I cup of the sugar and the eggs until very light and fluffy. Mix in the whipped cream.

2 Peel the peaches and remove the pits. Mash the peaches with a potato masher.

3 Add the mashed peaches to the egg and sugar mixture. Add the remaining I cup sugar and mix well. Stir in the remaining 2 cups heavy cream. Pour the mixture into a I-gallon ice-cream freezer. Freeze according to the manufacturer's directions.

MAKES 6 SERVINGS.

SUSAN GENTRY WILLIAMS (Nashville, Tennessee) says that her grandmother, **FLORA LETT BRYANT** (Johnson City, Tennessee), was affectionately called Mom. "Mom put two big aluminum pots outside when it began to snow," Susan says. "When one pot was almost full (about four inches), she added cream from the top of the bottle. (Back then, milk was delivered to the front porch in glass bottles; the top third of each glass bottle contained real cream.) My grandmother added sugar and one teaspoon of real vanilla. Then she scooped snow from the second pot into it until it was less creamy and more frozen. We sat on stools in the kitchen and ate the snow cream with sugar cookies. I'm looking forward to making snow cream with my grandchildren this winter; I'll just substitute half-and-half for the pure cream."

---

10 cups fresh, clean
snow

1 cup sugar

1 teaspoon vanilla
extract

1 cup cream or milk

---

1 When it starts to snow, place a large, clean bowl outside to collect the flakes. When the bowl is full, stir in the sugar and vanilla. Stir in just enough milk for the desired thickness of ice cream you prefer. Serve at once.

MAKES 5 TO 6 SERVINGS.

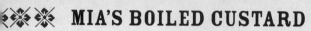 **MIA'S BOILED CUSTARD**

KELLY REYNOLDS (Nashville, Tennessee) says that her Mia turned ninety in 2010. Mia, **SARAH ELIZABETH JENKINS**, has lived all over the state of Tennessee. Kelly says, "Her daddy was a high school principal so they moved around a lot—Erwin, Bolliver, Knoxville—finally landing in Nashville for the past forty years. From the time I was born until I was sixteen, we lived next door to Mia. So all of my cooking and baking memories from my childhood include her. When I first started cooking on my own, I would always call her with simple questions like, 'How long do you boil carrots/potatoes?' And rather than give me the time in minutes, she would reply, 'Cook them until they are fork-tender.'"

2 ½ cups sugar

3 tablespoons all-purpose flour

6 large eggs, beaten

½ gallon milk

2 teaspoons vanilla extract

⅛ teaspoon ground nutmeg

1 Combine the sugar and flour in a saucepan. Combine the eggs and milk in a medium bowl and beat well. Gradually stir the egg mixture into the sugar mixture in the saucepan, stirring until smooth. Cook over medium heat, stirring constantly, until thick enough to coat a metal spoon. Be careful not to boil the mixture. Remove from the heat and stir in the vanilla and nutmeg.

2 Place a piece of plastic wrap over the surface of the custard to keep it from forming a skin. Cool the custard to room temperature. Pour the custard into a serving bowl or individual dishes. Cover and refrigerate for at least 3 hours before serving. Serve cool.

MAKES 12 TO 15 SERVINGS.

PECAN PRALINES

AVERY CLAIRE HAMPTON (Mount Juliet, Tennessee) says that her Maw-Maw, **SHARYN KAY PLYLAR WILLIAMS** (Biloxi, Mississippi), has a pantry and cabinets that are magic. Avery says, "No matter when we show up, she can always produce something sweet for us (much to the chagrin of our parents). These pralines are not the large sugary hunks that you pay two dollars for on the street in New Orleans or Gatlinburg—these are beautiful, small, caramel-colored morsels that are a delight to eat and share. And, Maw-Maw's pecan pralines make great gifts at the holidays. Enjoy!"

I cup white sugar

I cup firmly packed brown sugar

I cup uniformly chopped pecans

1/2 cup evaporated milk

I tablespoon butter

I teaspoon vanilla extract

1 In a medium saucepan combine the white sugar, brown sugar, pecans, and milk. Bring to a boil and cook for I to 2 minutes, until the mixture reaches the soft-ball stage. (If you put a drop of the cooked mixture into a cup of cold water and it forms a soft ball, the mixture is ready.) Remove the saucepan from the heat and add the butter and vanilla. Beat the candy by hand until the mixture starts to thicken and stick to the side of the pan. (Underbeating the candy mixture will cause the candy not to set. Overbeating the candy mixture will cause the candy to be cloudy and sugary.)

2 Drop the candy by teaspoonfuls onto wax paper. Allow to set for 60 minutes, then lift the wax paper and carefully peel it away from the pralines.

MAKES 2 DOZEN SMALL PRALINES.

PUMPKIN ROLL

AMANDA AUSTIN (Lafayette, Tennessee) says that her grandma, **JUANITA PRICE**, was born in Ashland, Kentucky, and later lived in Lafayette, Tennessee. "I always enjoyed cooking and baking with Grandma." Amanda says. "She, my mom, and I would make a day out of making these pumpkin rolls for everyone for Christmas—it was our tradition."

CAKE:

3 large eggs

2/3 cup canned pumpkin

1 cup white sugar

1 teaspoon salt

1 teaspoon soda

2 teaspoons ground cinnamon

2/3 cup all-purpose flour

1/3 cup chopped walnuts

powdered sugar for dusting

FILLING:

1 package (8 ounces) cream cheese

2 tablespoons butter

1 teaspoon vanilla extract

1 cup powdered sugar

1 Preheat the oven to 375 degrees.

2 **TO MAKE THE CAKE**, in a large bowl combine the eggs, pumpkin, white sugar, salt, soda, cinnamon, and flour and mix well.

3 Grease a 15 x 10 inch jelly roll pan, line it with wax paper, and grease the wax paper. Spread the dough onto the wax paper. Sprinkle the dough with the walnuts.

4 Bake for 15 minutes. After removing the pan from the oven, turn it upside down onto a towel that has been sprinkled with powdered sugar. Peel the wax paper off the cake. Place the towel with the sugared dough on it in the refrigerator to cool approximately 25 minutes.

5 **TO MAKE THE FILLING**, combine the cream cheese, butter, vanilla, and powdered sugar in a small bowl and mix until smooth. Spread the filling on the cooled cake and roll it up like a jelly roll. Place in the freezer for 24 hours before serving.

MAKES 14 TO 16 SERVINGS.

◆✖✖ BUG'S TOFFEE

MARY LOUISE "LOU" REYNOLDS (Nashville, Tennessee) is known for her desserts. Her family always looks forward to enjoying her toffee, cakes, and cookies. Granddaughters **ELIZABETH** and **MADELINE REYNOLDS** (also of Nashville) call her Memaw. They think it's funny that the four brothers Memaw grew up with nicknamed her Bug.

I cup almonds	3 tablespoons water	2 sticks butter
I ⅓ cups sugar	I tablespoon light corn syrup	I cup semisweet chocolate chips

---

1 Preheat the oven to 350 degrees.

2 Blanch, peel, roast, and chop the almonds. To blanch the almonds, place them in a bowl. Pour boiling water to barely cover almonds. Let the almonds sit for exactly I minute, but no longer. Drain, rinse under cold water, and drain again. Pat the almonds dry and slip the skins off. To roast the almonds, spread the skinned nuts on an ungreased cookie sheet and bake for 10 to 12 minutes. When cool, chop the almonds and set aside.

3 In a medium saucepan, cook the sugar, water, corn syrup, and butter in a saucepan over low heat until the mixture reaches 300 degrees, as measured with a candy thermometer. Add half of the chopped almonds and mix well.

4 Spread the toffee mixture on a 15 x 10-inch greased jelly-roll pan. Sprinkle the chocolate chips on top of the toffee. Let the chocolate chips sit for 45 seconds to melt a bit and then spread them across the toffee, distributing them evenly. Sprinkle the remaining almonds on top. Place the pan in the freezer for 10 to 15 minutes to set and cool. Break the toffee into pieces before serving.

MAKES 1 TO 2 POUNDS.

CHOCOLATE DATE-NUT BARS

HANNAH TURNER LAVEY (Nashville Tennessee) shares that her Grandmama, **BERNICE WILLIAMS HIGHTOWER**, was the most amazing cook. "I loved as a child to sit out in her screened porch and help her shell butter beans and field peas or peel peaches over her deep kitchen sink," Hannah says. "She did everything carefully and precisely. She had a huge standing freezer right in her kitchen that was always full of summer vegetables, her famous stuffed potatoes (my personal favorite), and casseroles. And there was always a cake or pie on the counter. Grandmama stood over her 1951 stove until her very last days, stirring a small pot of butter beans or cheese grits and always adding a heap of salt. My grandmother, and now my mother, is famous for these chocolate date-nut bars."

---

1 stick butter

1 heaping tablespoon cocoa

1 cup sugar

2 eggs, lightly beaten

2/3 cup all-purpose flour

1 teaspoon vanilla extract

1/2 cup chopped dates

1/2 cup chopped pecans

shortening for greasing the pan

powdered sugar for dusting

---

1 Preheat the oven to 350 degrees.

2 Melt the butter in a saucepan over low heat. When melted, add the cocoa and sugar, continuing to cook until well mixed. Remove from the heat. Add the eggs and mix well. Stir in the flour. Add the vanilla, dates, and pecans and mix well. Line an 8-inch square baking pan with wax paper. Coat the wax paper with shortening on the top side only. Pour the batter into the pan.

3 Bake for 20 to 30 minutes. Invert the bars onto wax paper coated with powdered sugar. Peel off the wax paper from the top and dust with more powdered sugar on the top. Cool the bars on a wire rack and cut into squares.

MAKES 40 TO 50 BARS.

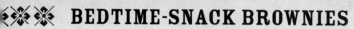

BEDTIME-SNACK BROWNIES

"Brownies and milk were my favorite bedtime snack whenever I spent the night at my grandparents' house," says **WENDY NEWTON** (Nashville, Tennessee). "I called them Pap and Sissy." Sissy is **SYLVIA EASTERBERG** (Johnson City, Tennessee). "Sissy would always have the best treats at her house," Wendy says. "I'd help her make brownies, cakes, and cookies, and my favorite part was when we were done and I got to lick the spoon and anything that was left in the bowl. To this day, whenever I eat a brownie, I think of Sissy and the irreplaceable moments we shared."

---

1 ½ cups margarine

6 squares (1 ounce each) unsweetened baking chocolate

3 cups sugar

6 large eggs

1 ½ cups all-purpose flour

1 ½ teaspoons vanilla extract

3/4 teaspoon salt

1 cup chopped pecans

---

1 Preheat the oven to 350 degrees.

2 Melt the margarine and chocolate in a saucepan, stirring constantly. Remove from the heat and stir in the sugar. Beat in the eggs one at a time. Add the flour, vanilla, salt, and pecans and mix well. Spoon the batter into a greased and floured 13 x 9-inch baking pan.

3 Bake for 35 to 40 minutes, or until a toothpick inserted in the center comes out clean. Cool on a wire rack and cut into squares.

MAKES 4 DOZEN BROWNIES.

K. K.'S FOUR-CHIP FUDGE

MANDY HELTSLEY BUTTERS (Nashville, Tennessee) says that her grandmother, K. K., **KATHERINE KEELING** (also of Nashville), lived on a farm with two brothers. They used to ride horses to school every day. One day, she and her brothers tied their dad's expensive new milking bucket to her horse's tail and then they put apples in the bucket. The bucket pulled on the horse's tail and it bucked K. K. and the bucket off, shattering the new bucket all to pieces. Needless to say, their dad was pretty upset. They had an orchard in Wartrace, Tennessee, with peaches, apples, Bing cherries, grapes, and pears. Because of the farm, they had produce to eat year round. They'd wrap apples and pears in brown paper and put them in the basement and they'd last forever. They also dried some of the fruit for Southern fried pies.

---

1 1/2 sticks plus 1 1/2 teaspoons butter, divided

3 tablespoons milk

1 can (14 ounces) sweetened condensed milk

1 package (12 ounces) semisweet chocolate chips

1 package (11.5 ounces) milk chocolate chips

1 cup butterscotch-flavored chips

1 package (10 ounces) peanut butter–flavored chips

1 1/2 teaspoons vanilla extract

2 teaspoons almond extract

1 jar (7 ounces) marshmallow crème

1 pound chopped walnuts

---

1 Line a 13 x 9-inch pan with foil. Grease the foil with 1 1/2 teaspoons of butter and set aside.

2 Melt the remaining butter in a medium saucepan pan over low heat. Stir in the milk and the condensed milk. Add the semisweet, milk chocolate, butterscotch, and peanut butter chips and cook, stirring constantly, until smooth. Remove from the heat. Stir in the vanilla extract, almond extract, and marshmallow crème. Stir in the walnuts.

3 Spoon the mixture into the foiled pan and spread evenly. Cover and chill in the refrigerator until firm. Cut into squares. Store in the refrigerator in an airtight container.

MAKES 4 TO 5 POUNDS.

Acknowledgments

Thank you to Joe Porter, Violet Cieri, Jamie Chavez, Pam Laxton, Heather Donahoe, Stephanie Tresner, Danielle Bolen, and Rosie Colvin for testing recipes.

A special thank you to Susan Hagenau and Pam Laxton for preparing food for the photo shoot, and to Ron Manville and Teresa Blackburn for making it all look so beautiful.

About the Author

Prior to 1997, Faye had visited certain Southern cities either for vacation, or en route to another destination for work or fun. However, in May of 1997, two of her three brothers relocated to Nashville and her love affair with this part of the South began. After they moved, missing them and visiting often, Faye decided it was time for her to relocate as well. While it took a while for a Chicago-based girl to find a Tennessee job, by January of the new millennium, she had made a fresh start in Nashville. And the rest, as they say, is history. Faye says she has never looked back and has never, even for a minute, second-guessed her decision to move south.

The warmth and welcome of the people, the hills and lush green surroundings remind her of Pennsylvania, where she was born. And the food? In the South, comfort food abounds. Faye shares that what tickled her most was her first trip to a meat 'n' three. "A what?" she remembers asking when a Southern coworker (now a great friend) invited her to lunch. She was amazed by the food. It was just like a childhood Sunday dinner at Grandma's—real down-home cooking at its best—but it was offered seven days a week! And the best part was that in the South, macaroni and cheese is a vegetable! (Many restaurants of the meat 'n' three persuasion list it under the vegetable selections.) Faye knew that her food life couldn't get much better than that!

Faye's background includes more than twenty years of experience in communications and in marketing- and education-related capacities in corporate and nonprofit settings. Her publishing background includes managing editor roles for *MyBusiness* magazine (published by the National Federation of Independent Business) and *Real Estate Issues* (a commercial real estate journal published by the Counselors of Real Estate). She is currently the executive editor of *The Source* magazine and the director of education and communications for HealthTrust Purchasing Group in Brentwood, Tennessee. And she's newly married to none other than a Southern gentleman.

Index

Contributor Index

Your Family Recipes